# YOU'RE NOT BROKEN

# YOU'RE
# NOT
# BROKEN

5 STEPS TO BECOME **SUPERCONSCIOUS**

AND **ACTIVATE YOUR MAGIC**

CHRISTOPHER MICHAEL DUNCAN

**DUNCAN** PUBLISHING

YOU'RE NOT BROKEN

*5 Steps to Become Superconscious and Activate Your Magic*

ISBN   978-1-5445-1944-9  *Hardcover*

978-1-5445-1943-2  *Paperback*

978-1-5445-1942-5  *Ebook*

978-1-5445-1945-6  *Audiobook*

*To Deas, my brother, I miss you.*

# CONTENTS

ACKNOWLEDGMENTS.................................................................9

INTRODUCTION .....................................................................II

1. THE JOURNEY OF CREATING A LIFE YOU LOVE.....................27

2. THE CREATIVE ENERGY .........................................................45

3. INDIVIDUATION ....................................................................65

4. STRUCTURE ..........................................................................85

5. THE MAGNETIC MOMENT......................................................121

6. BECOMING SUPERCONSCIOUS..............................................151

7. TRUE CHOICES .....................................................................185

8. THE FIVE-STEP SUPERCONSCIOUS CREATOR CODE.............223

GAME TIME .............................................................................253

ABOUT THE AUTHOR...............................................................257

# ACKNOWLEDGMENTS

This book would not have happened without some amazing people helping me along the way. Here is a very small selection:

To my wife, thank you for everything. Thank you for your patience, support, and love to help this book and work come to life. I love you.

To my parents, thank you for giving me the best start in life. I love you.

To my teachers and mentors, especially Colette and William, thank you for your wisdom, guidance, and clarity. Without you, this book would not exist.

To my conscious education family, team, and clients, I am

so grateful to all of you. This is our book! We get to share this with the world! I am so proud of you.

And finally, thanks to you, the reader, who picked up this book in a conscious effort to create the best life possible. I love you!

# INTRODUCTION

What you hold in your hands is the definitive guide to creating a life you love, using your Superconscious.

You will learn to orient to the world in a new structure, allowing you to create amazing end results that you love. You will learn how to connect to the Superconscious field, transform any limitations, and magically manifest thoughts into things.

You will learn the simple Five-Step Process that only takes fifteen minutes a day and will create magical results in your life. You will learn how to connect to your Superconscious, manifest with ease, and remove any resistance to what you desire through the "Recode" process.

In order to write this book, I had to become it. I needed to live, breathe, and prove everything you are about to learn. I struggled deeply to integrate many of the concepts within, and I hope I communicate them in a way that is meaningful, practical, and easy to implement.

Science supports everything I write in this book. I draw on quantum physics, epigenetics, neuroscience, and ancient wisdom. Yet, this is not an academic paper; this is an operating manual, a plan, a new way of being.

This work is not just mine; it is a synthesis of years of research, trial, error, experience, and mastery passed down to me by many intelligent individuals. These people have coached, trained, and inspired me along the way, and my only hope is that I do their brilliance justice in this book.

This book is meant to be read from start to finish, in the order it is written. Many concepts and exercises build on each other. Each story and each exercise is coded in a specific pattern to ensure your Superconscious is awakened and engaged in the perfect way. Many ideas are repeated and re-explained in different ways to ensure all aspects of you understand exactly how to complete this amazing work.

What this book will do for you is quite literally out of this world, so do not take it lightly. This book will change your life, so don't skip through a section or an exercise. If you do not have time to do an exercise in the moment, just wait and come back to it when you do.

## THE WAKE-UP CALL

For years, I tried to create change by focusing on my conscious beliefs. I did mantras, used affirmations, and read countless books. I then graduated to working on my Unconscious or Subconscious beliefs and found better results.

It wasn't until tragedy struck in my life that I was introduced to the Superconscious field of information. Once I was introduced, it was all I heard about for the next four years. Finally, I gave in and accepted a new reality—one filled with intuition, genius, and power. This reality was in direct contrast to being a victim—a powerless and reactive person.

In March of 2016, my world changed. My business partner and very close friend, Mark Deason ("Deas" to me), was killed in a motorcycle crash. Not only was he running our company, but he was also the first mentor who introduced me to the world of self-development. He was my number one support, besides my wife, and my closest confidant.

In the ten years before he died, I went from being a DJ at his bar to hiring him into my company. I had Deas run operations, and we eventually became full partners. Not a day went by when we didn't talk. We had plans to change the world through our business, and in one moment, those plans were all gone.

I distinctly remember the moment I found out he had died. I was at an event in Anaheim, California, where I was promoting a big-name speaker, with over 200 people in attendance. I was frantically running around making sure everyone was being looked after; however, my phone would not stop buzzing.

I finally picked it up to hear Dave (Deas' roommate in Bali) on the other end of the phone, letting me know that Deas had died hours ago in a motorcycle accident. I was listed as the person to call in the case of an accident. I then had the grim task of informing his family. There has never been a harder moment in my life.

The months that followed were excruciating. The business fell apart, and I fell apart emotionally. It felt like the world had been ripped from me. All my plans for the future seemed pointless. How could life be so cruel? And what was the point of it all, anyway? Falling from a multimillion-dollar business to hundreds of thousands in debt over a period of just a few months was not pleasant. Losing my support, my friend, and my mentor was even harder.

Many of my other friends reached out to help. Many offered

for me to attend their healing seminars, have free sessions, or even go on retreats at no cost. But I didn't feel like doing any work. I had given up.

Previous to this collapse, I had been flying high, traveling the world and speaking in over a dozen countries to thousands of people at live events. I had even been invited to be featured in a movie called *Rise Up* with a star-studded cast, including Anthony Robbins, the Dalai Lama, and more.

As I flew back to LA for the filming, I was flooded with messages from a lady named Colette, who apparently had a new healing method she wanted to show me. I wanted nothing of it. However, she insisted we meet up after filming since she was in LA, too, and I reluctantly agreed.

I sat down for the first session with Colette with a sense of "I don't want to be here." She spent thirty minutes explaining what the Superconscious was and how it works to create fast change. She explained memory structures and where our beliefs come from; then she asked me to do a test session to learn the process based on a fear, "Maybe you have a fear of public speaking?" she said.

"Ha ha, no way," I replied. "I love public speaking."

She kept digging.

After a painful minute of silence, I shared that I had worked on everything and was fine—everything except my anger at the world for my circumstances.

She decided we would work through that anger. I had this huge chip on my shoulder. I was mad at my friend for dying. I was stressed trying to do the right thing by his family, look after my staff, and keep all my promises to my customers. I had to admit I was doing a terrible job with all of it, and I was making unbelievably stupid business decisions. I was a mess.

Colette asked me to close my eyes, and she began working with my Superconscious by asking some questions and giving strange commands. It all seemed stupid and like a watered-down version of neuro-linguistic programming (NLP) or hypnosis. I wasn't impressed until it hit me.

I suddenly felt a huge sense of fear come over me. It rattled through my body, creating some very odd muscle movements.

Then SNAP, it was gone.

It felt like my brain had just let go of whatever the problem was. Like it was actually gone.

"What was I so upset about?" I said, laughing out loud.

I had gone from being totally upset about my friend and my circumstances to calm in just minutes. I couldn't make sense of it. I was asked to open my eyes, and I sat there, stunned and in awe. This was the beginning of a lifelong friendship with Colette and an obsession with the Superconscious.

For two years, I worked with the Superconscious every day. I did one-on-one sessions with Colette multiple times a week to clear everything that was in the way. I had my staff take sessions and even launched business programs with Colette to get her work out into the world.

I got amazing results, but I couldn't keep the momentum going for long. Luckily, I met the only other person in the world who could help me see I was only exercising the Superconscious for half of what it could do.

This chance encounter happened when I flew to London to run a workshop on public speaking. During the workshop, I was having fun using Superconscious commands to play with public speaking fears in the audience when a woman said, "This reminds me of William Whitecloud. Do you know him?"

I had met William eight years before this moment, at a high-priced, intimate workshop for business owners. I didn't know I was sitting next to the best-selling author of

*The Magician's Way* at the time. We never really formed a bond, other than connecting on Facebook, so I replied, "No, I don't really know him."

The woman's reply changed my life. "You really need to connect with him. He does this work as well."

For some reason, I couldn't shake off what she said. I had to connect with William. Later that night, I reached out on Facebook, letting him know I really had to speak to him. I think I sent four or five messages within twenty-four hours, with a request for us to get on a call. I must have sounded crazy as his reply was, "Are you alright, amigo?" His response still makes me laugh today.

He was busy and didn't have spare time to indulge people he hardly knew. He asked me to read his books, and then we'd speak within a week.

Happy with his answer, I went to Amazon and purchased both of his books. On the flight home from London to Australia, I read them twice. Here was the missing link. He wrote about creating, intuition, magic, and how to use the Superconscious to create. I couldn't believe it.

When I finally got to speak to William, we connected instantly. We both had studied Robert Fritz's work and were applying it in different ways. William used it to create, and I used it in sales and public speaking.

We made a decision: I would help him with online marketing, and he would coach me on how to connect to my genius intelligence and intuition using the Superconscious.

I was hooked. I worked with him twice a month and attended his complete training curriculum, which taught psychic ability, intuition, alchemy, and much more.

From that moment on, everything sped up. Within the next two years, I earned more money than I had ever made, married the love of my life, created my dream house, and became the happiest I had ever been. It seemed I finally got what I was searching for. The combination of my earlier discovery, structure, and all the aspects of the Superconscious turned me into a manifesting powerhouse.

I started to understand the Superconscious and created a working relationship with it. I began to get clear interpretations of myself and others, and I found that I could communicate with their Superconscious to create huge transformations.

I stopped having Colette work with my team and me, and I started performing the sessions myself using a combination of the things I had learned over the past fifteen years. The results were amazing.

One day, I was sitting doing my morning meditation, connecting to the Superconscious, and asking for guidance. I was given clear instructions to "put on a workshop and teach a Recode."

I had no idea what the Recode was, but I had a vision I was on stage working with people and using this new method. So, I told my team and my wife we were going to do an evening session on the Superconscious Recode, and I was going to bring people up on stage and demonstrate it.

I scheduled three events, one on the Gold Coast, one in Brisbane, and one on the Sunshine Coast. I was nervous about doing the first one, but I'm glad I followed through.

The video recording of that session shows me working with two women in front of the audience and "Recoding" their fear of public speaking in minutes. The women shifted from shaking and nervousness to complete confidence and calm. This video was the catalyst for a movement that is now generating over $1 million in sales a month and has over 10,000 happy clients globally.

It is totally magic!

If you have been on a journey to create a life you love, transform your health, or manifest something new in your life, this is your wake-up call.

You are not broken; you do not need to fix yourself.

You are Superconscious.

## WHAT IS YOUR SUPERCONSCIOUS?

Your Superconscious is an aspect of you, which is more "You" than anything you think you are. It is one of the three aspects of the mind we will discuss in this book. The Superconscious is where your innate genius, intuition, and universal connection is. Up until now, you have likely not had a functional working relationship with this part of yourself and, therefore, have only ever experienced yourself as limited.

It's time to change that.

Creating a working relationship with the Superconscious will allow you to create beautiful end results, turn your thoughts into things with predictability, create amazing healing transformations, and harness the magic of manifestation.

Along with being guided by coaches, mentors, and teachers,

I have studied and applied success education and personal development. Altogether, my experience has proven to me the validity of using my Superconscious mind to create anything my heart desires in this world.

Before I say more about the Superconscious, you must understand how much we have been misled and misguided. We have had our natural power taken away from us. It has been handed over to others—to pills, education, institutions, and leaders who do not know the truth. In this book, you will find the truth.

The truth is you are a powerful creator of everything in your reality. You are not broken.

If you have ever been to a conference or seminar or read a book that promises you will create a better life, you likely have been misled. You were likely told there was something to fix or improve about yourself or that there was something you must do to become a success.

The focus on needing to fix, improve, or heal our current reality is actually the problem. This focus causes more pain than you can imagine.

In this book, you will discover the truth that you do not need to fix, improve, or heal yourself in order to create a life you love. I will explain, in detail, how many structures in society work against us and prevent us from creating a life we love and how to step outside of those structures. I will also share secrets that have been hidden for centuries and give you a step-by-step code to use your Superconscious to create magic.

I am so happy to be your guide on the journey to magical manifestation and creating beautiful end results that you love.

For me, this was such a huge breakthrough, and it only happened after I "lost it all" when my best friend died. At the moment of losing it all—my best friend, my business, my success, my emotions—I discovered something important. I could choose to feel good. I didn't have to be a powerless victim. I could smile and love my life. I could live my purpose and be healthy.

I still remember the moment I "opened the gate" and realized I was not just a limited perspective—I was Superconscious awareness and was creating everything. I remember feeling as though I was breathing the universe, and at the same time, it was breathing me. I was the observed and the observer. In this moment, I realized I was connected to everything, and I was not separate. This changed everything.

This realization was the biggest gift, but it took another two years to fully accept the moment and to reorient myself.

The Five-Step Superconscious Creator Code I share in this book will teach you how to connect to these end results, notice any resistance you have created to their manifestation, and then change the instructions that caused the resistance. This will remove the resistance and allow the correct action to flow.

The action that will flow could be an internal action like a health transformation, or it could be an external action like going out and starting a business.

As a creative energy, you will always take the path of least resistance. However, you created all resistance as a useful barrier in an attempt to avoid pain. If you experienced a negative outcome, your Superconscious would create a blockage to stop it from happening in the future. Think of it like putting a dam in the way of a stream. No flow can happen until the dam is opened. By Recoding, you open the dam.

This journey, and what I will share with you in this book, changed my life. Thousands have used it to create miraculous healing transformations, to manifest more money, abundance, or better futures, and to turn dreams into reality. With this book, you will unlock the secret genie within and become a powerful creator.

## WHAT TO EXPECT

By the end of reading this book, you will know the Superconscious Creator Code, a five-step method that allows you
to get into the correct structure to unlock your natural gifts,
intuition, and genius and create a magnetic mind, pulling
in anything you really desire.

This book is a challenge, a call to action. I will ask you to
step into a new reality to reconsider some of your deepest-
held beliefs and will give you a second chance in life. I will
give you the code, but you will have to use it, implement it,
and assimilate it to make it your own.

Many who find their way to this work have spent a lifetime
(or lifetimes) seeking to understand how to create what they
love and have found themselves going around in circles.
This is where the journey of seeking stops and where a new
life will emerge, so treasure what you find here.

It is time to create a life you love.

# CHAPTER 1

---

# THE JOURNEY
# OF CREATING A
# LIFE YOU LOVE

As humans, we all go on a predictable journey, don't we?
While growing up, I saw most adults living the same experiences, and to my childlike worldview, their lives seemed
dull, boring, and lifeless. I always had a sense there was
more, and it took fifteen years of my adult life to discover
just how much more there is.

Many of us have asked the questions: "Why are we here?"
or "What is the meaning of life?" We find ourselves lost or
confused. Is our life really about finding a good job, getting
married, and raising a family? Surely, there has to be more.

All humans start off in the same place—as a pure creative energy. The unfortunate thing is most people never reach their full potential as creators. They stay stuck in an oscillating pattern, never reaching a life they love, and always in a struggle with themselves and the world. It doesn't seem to matter how much "work they do on themselves" or how many books they read; they seem to only be able to create short-term progress in one area of life and come crashing back to "reality" in others.

Why don't we all have everything we desire? Are we born to just struggle from birth to death?

You may feel like you have an internal conflict going on from choosing between:

- what you love to create and what you actually experience in life.
- going for it and playing it safe.
- being your authentic self and conforming to others' expectations.
- self-confidence and self-doubt

I have found most people are settling in certain areas of life. They've stopped dreaming, stopped going for it, and settled into predictable patterns.

I get it. It can be difficult to know what you should really go for. I also know that if you are reading this book, you are one of the few who have identified this pattern and decided you want more.

## OBSTACLES TO THE LIFE YOU LOVE

You may have even made the decision to "go for more" long ago, and you've been on a lifelong journey to achieve the "dream life." You progressed in some areas and remained stagnant in others. I have worked with thousands of people in my coaching and workshops. Nearly all of them desire to create more success in their life, but for some reason, they have not. After all this time, I have found three big problems that nearly everyone struggles with:

### I. THEY ARE IN A PROBLEM/POWERLESS STRUCTURE WITH WHAT THEY DESIRE.

They have given the power to outside conditions. Some make them feel good—a relationship, health, money, and status. Some make them feel bad—failure, rejection, judgment, bad health, and being single. This structure, as you will learn, is the biggest problem for people who desire big transformation. You must get out of the oscillating structure and into a flowing structure, where every end result you go for is easy to move towards, achieve, and keep for the long term.

## 2. THEY DON'T ACTUALLY WANT WHAT THEY THINK THEY WANT.

They don't actually want the business; they want to love their day. They don't actually want the sports car; they want respect. They don't know what they truly desire. They have never been allowed to simply connect to what they love and create a life based on that. Instead, others have told them what to go for—the media, parents, society, peers, and worst of all, personal development speakers who make them write down worthless crap they think they want. They are told to "dream bigger" rather than to find what they really love.

I have one rule when it comes to deciding what you really want to create: that you would love to see it created. That's it. If there are other reasons, you are not in a true choice! Create end results that you love; no other reason is needed.

This may seem very different than what you were told growing up or what you see in the world. Most people are really only going for things they believe will get them somewhere better or will solve a problem. Most are not creating a life they love.

## 3. THEY HAVE FORGOTTEN WHO AND WHAT THEY REALLY ARE—A PURE CREATIVE ENERGY THAT HAS ALREADY DECIDED AND CREATED EVERYTHING.

Most are not living from the truth of what they are—their power is given away, and they feel powerless to circumstances and conditions. There is always something against them. There is always something to fight—health challenges, relationship problems, the government, or society. So, they decide to fight this imaginary enemy by using outside forces—people, relationships, medication, education, drugs, seminars, workshops, or therapy, only to find any real change that occurs is due to reconnecting to the creative energy they really are.

To get over these obstacles, you will need to realize you are Superconscious. When you learn to create from the Superconscious, you have access to all the knowledge there has ever been. You can Recode original instructions, manifest miraculous transformations, and be the powerful creator you always were.

## FROM PREDICTABLE PATH TO SUPERCONSCIOUS CREATOR

In our society, we all follow a predictable path. When you decide to become a Superconscious creator, you make the "shift" as shown in this illustration.

# THE JOURNEY TO
# SUPERCONSCIOUS LIVING

9. Become Superconscious, live your truth, have it all now, and create more of what you love.

1. Pure Creative Spirit

2. Become an individual with a limited perspective.

8. Recode all resistance and follow through. Turn thoughts into things.

3. Orientate to the world through this limitation.

**Connect to your Superconscious.**

7. Use your Superconscious insight to make true choices you love.

4. Create your life to solve your limitation and create oscillation.

6. Recode all the instructions causing resistance to having it now. Live the Core 4.

5. Decide to become a creator and live the Core 4 choices.

Powerful Superconscious creator of your reality.

**The Shift**

Powerless, self-conscious victim to circumstance.

The following is a brief breakdown of this journey.

## I. CREATIVE ENERGY

We all start out having it all. We are a pure creative energy connected to the unified field of all possibilities. Our mothers carry us around in the womb, and we have everything—food, water, oxygen...everything.

Then suddenly, we realize we do not have it all simply by existing. We realize we are an individual who is separate from others.

## 2. INDIVIDUATION

When we are born, we become an individual. Now, we have to do something to get enough food and water to ensure our survival. We realize we can do something to get love/ attention from our parents, and we can do something to lose it. We realize there is a "way to be" that is successful. We believe there's a way to be a better human (more validated) and a way to be less than.

We learn that if we do something good, we get praise; if we do something bad, we get told off.

We realize what is good and bad.

We learn what is right and wrong.

We learn how to ensure we get mum's love and dad's praise.

This loss of "having it all" is very painful and unacceptable. To make sense of this new world, we make up beliefs about ourselves to ease the pain.

These beliefs create our orientation to the world and can sound like:

If I just _____ then I will achieve/be/have _____.

If I just _____ then I will avoid _____.

### 3. STUCK IN A POWERLESS/PROBLEM ORIENTATION

Because of our focus on how we are limited, we set up a worldview that our life is about completing ourselves or solving the negative beliefs/limitations.

There are six sabotaging beliefs that cause huge problems for people who want to create a life they love. We will cover these in Chapter 3. These beliefs are the underlying structure of all motivation, and it becomes our life purpose to resolve them. However, in the attempt to overcome the belief, our identity gets caught in the belief, and we can never truly escape it.

For example, if you didn't get attention growing up except for when you did something amazing, you may decide you are not worthy of love/attention just the way you are and set up a structure to do amazing things to finally prove you are worthy. You will get really motivated and set a big goal, and move towards it. However, as soon as you get close to achieving it, you will find a way to sabotage it.

This is a setup. You don't achieve your goal because if you were to actually "make it," you would have to accept you are worthy, and your former identity would be lost; you would no longer know who you are.

Your identity gets wrapped up in the not-worthy view. You never accept your worth and spend a lifetime chasing a moving goal post when what you really wanted was available the whole time.

This example reflects the oscillating pattern in people's lives. They simply have an identity conflict, and their results move back and forth like a pendulum.

With a powerless/problem-orientation, they can never solve the negative belief about themselves. If they were no longer "not good enough," who would they be? Conversely, they can never truly be not good enough because that is far too painful, so they live somewhere in the middle.

Does this sound familiar? Stuck in the middle, never fully being not good enough and never fully feeling good enough.

Each of the six sabotaging beliefs works in a similar way; they keep us stuck in patterns, unable to have what we desire.

The more you try to resolve a way in which you feel incomplete, the more you give your power away and stay stuck in an oscillating pattern. The more you try to fix it, the worse it gets.

There is a real, big problem with the problem-orientation.

## 4. THE CREATIVE ORIENTATION

The only way to move towards your goals without sabotage is to let go of that structure.

The first thing you must do is get in the correct structure. You will learn how in Chapter 5.

In short, you must learn to let go of the old structure and create a new way of being in the world. You must define yourself as a powerful creator, not a powerless victim. This is the big TURNING POINT.

You do not need to be anything other than who you are to create everything you desire.

You are the creative spirit who created everything you have in your life. You have just forgotten.

You must connect to your Superconscious and create a new set of instructions for your Unconscious to follow. You must learn to Recode all resistance so you can have it all now.

This is the first step—to orient from a place of power!

You can have everything you desire now! EVERYTHING!!! And you can still be motivated to create more.

Most people think if they had everything now, they would no longer be motivated because their whole lives have been about overcoming problems.

However, *this belief* is the problem.

Once you realize and accept you can have everything you want now—abundance, love, joy, family, health, and fun— and you fully understand that you create it all, you will realize that:

- You can't do anything to be more worthy.
- You can't do anything to be more or less enough.
- You can't be more significant.
- You can't be more capable.
- You can't belong more.
- You are perfect now.

When we connect with the Superconscious, we realize we

actually have it all already, and there is no need to solve or fix anything. From this perspective, we can choose or Recode any belief structures to fit with the life we desire. The truth you will find is that you can have it all now and still be motivated to create what you love. You can actually choose what you would love to create because you are no longer problem-solving.

Before this moment, everything you did was in service of a "better" future. As soon as you believe there is a better future, you have fallen back into a problem-orientation. Letting go of the problem-orientation is not easy. I have seen people struggle for months, even years, to make the shift, but shifting into the "creative orientation" is the first step to becoming a Superconscious creator. To shift into the creative orientation, you come from a place of already having what you desire, instead of a place of lack or problem-solving. To be in the creative orientation, you must BE it to SEE it. You must become "it" before it comes to be. Being whole now is the goal now.

You must let go of the childish wound and desire to finally validate yourself in this world.

There is nothing you can do to be more or less. You, me, and every other human have the same value.

In this book, I will reference the "wizard's gate," a term that describes the process of opening to the present moment. It is like a doorway of your perception, where you drop into your heart-awareness, or innocence, and become connected to your Superconscious. When you go through the wizard's gate, there is nothing that can make life better. You have reconnected to the unified field. You are everything. From this point, you can shift and change any instructions you have coded into your reality, and you can access Superconscious awareness.

The wizard's gate is the perfect metaphor to explain what you must do to step into a new reality and accept the magnetic moment—the moment when you have everything now and create from a place of already being what you desire. Again, this is not about problem-solving. We leave that old reality behind.

This is the shift or turning point that takes you from the powerless orientation to the powerful orientation. It is the second big move towards creating a life you love.

You claim the magnetic moment.

The magnetic moment is when you have everything you desire NOW. You have become "it." You have become the person who is 100 percent in alignment with your desire.

You can absolutely be happy now, fully satisfied in life, and inspired to create more.

Many people have only ever been motivated to do something based on how it will improve their life; by claiming the magnetic moment, you have it all now and let go of your old structure.

Luckily, you hold in your hands the fastest and easiest way to do this. As we go through this process, you will see how the NOW can be EVERYTHING you could ever ask for, and included in that NOW is the ability to create something you love, just because you love it.

You can reorient and create a new structure, one that easily sails to the destination you desire while enjoying every minute.

You must learn to connect to your Superconscious and Recode the instructions.

You must stop the self-sabotage/worry/fear.

You can create what you love, knowing NOTHING will give or take away your core satisfaction in life.

## 6. CREATE YOUR TRUE END RESULTS

There are many things you could focus on creating in this lifetime, but only some of them are what you truly love. Creating what you love is our priority. To do so, we will first focus on creating the magnetic moment, so you are in a creative orientation and not problem-solving.

You may need to focus on making this shift for a number of months because you have been in the problem-orientation for decades. The old patterns are hard-wired into your neurology. You must open the gate and have it all now. Only then can you create from a place of no resistance and not fight your identity the whole way.

To enter the magnetic moment and step into the new structure, you need to make four core choices as a Superconscious creator. The four core choices to reorient yourself are:

- I choose to live my true nature and purpose.
- I choose to be the predominant creative force in my life.
- I choose to live a life I love.
- I choose to be healthy and vital.

Until you are living these four, you won't be ready to move to the second level of Superconscious creation. These are the basic building blocks to create the structure that allows flow to happen.

Every single person on the planet can choose these four now. They are not problem-solving. They create:

- A new reality.
- A new structure.
- A new orientation.

Once you have "mastered the magnetic moment" and are living the core four choices, it is time to tune into what you would really love to create. Now, life gets magical!

What would you really love to create for no reason other than you would just love to have it?

This is your truth. This is why you are on the planet, and there is nothing more fulfilling than turning your highest desires/loves into reality. Life becomes so much fun!

## 7. LIVING A SUPERCONSCIOUS LIFE

Now you have the ability to turn thoughts into things. You have entered the wizard's gate and connected to the moment. You are truly satisfied with what you have and are in joy creating more. Life is fun.

Now you can follow a few core principles and structures to make creating your end results even easier.

You get to use the Five-Step Superconscious Creator Code in many different ways. You will use it in a specific way each day and each week, removing resistance and taking action. Each month, quarter, and year, you will use it to get clear insight and intuition on where you should be going and to ensure what you are creating is a true choice.

Living this way is a gift and full of wonderful surprises. You will have it all and be able to manifest anything and everything you truly desire!

Now that you know the journey and where we are going, it's time to understand each step and exactly how to make it happen. Let's get straight into the next chapter to really understand what the Superconscious is.

## CHAPTER 1 REVIEW

We are all on a similar human journey. Most people get stuck in their limited perspective and create a life of oscillation. This is because they are trying to resolve their identity and feel complete.

Focusing on problem-solving leads to a life of problems.

You must learn to let go of the old structure and create a new way of being in the world. You must define yourself as a powerful creator, not a powerless victim. This is the big TURNING POINT.

You do not need to create based on solving a problem or making the future better. The NOW can be EVERYTHING you could ever ask for.

The four core choices to reorient yourself are:

1.  I choose to live my true nature and purpose.
2.  I choose to be the predominant creative force in my life.
3.  I choose to live a life I love.
4.  I choose to be healthy and vital.

The Five-Step Superconscious Creator Code allows you to create what you love—fast.

# CHAPTER 2

——◆——

# THE CREATIVE ENERGY

In this chapter, I will focus on the science of how this process works. If science is not your thing, don't worry. Read with an open mind. I have kept it light, and I promise you don't need a PhD to get through this.

The new science of quantum physics and unified field theory is finally catching up to what religious and spiritual teachers have known for thousands of years—we are far more than blood and flesh and bone. This science can help explain what we witness every day when working with the Superconscious.

Until now, biology and physics were based on views created by Isaac Newton, the father of modern physics. Everything we believed about our world and our place within it reflected his ideas. Newton presented the theory that all the elements of the universe are isolated from each other, divisible, and wholly self-contained; he created a world-view of separateness.

For Newton, the material world was made of individual particles of matter that followed certain laws of motion through space and time. The world was composed of a load of little discrete objects which behaved predictably. In his view, the universe was just a big machine. The most separate of all was the human being, who sat outside this universe looking in.

The problem with his theories is at the quantum level; they do not reflect what we observe. The theories make sense for the "big things," like animals, planets, and solar systems, but do not hold up at the sub-atomic level, which is what the big things are made of. Somehow, we have one set of rules for the big things and another set of rules for what they are made of. It just doesn't sound right, does it?

Luckily, many well-respected scientists all over the world have been carrying out well-designed experiments, and the results fly in the face of current biology and physics. Together, these studies offer us copious information about the central organizing force that governs our bodies and the rest of the universe.

## SCIENCE IS CATCHING UP

What has been discovered is wonderful and confirms what many of you know to be true in your heart, at your deepest, most fundamental level: we are not a chemical reaction but an energetic charge. This pulsating energy charge is the central engine of our being and our consciousness.

Because of the field of quantum physics, science is able to prove many of the ideas that spiritual masters have been teaching for years. In fact, many of the founders of quantum physics were very interested in spirituality and obsessed with using science to validate it. We are finally bridging the gaps between science, spirituality, and what we observe in our physical reality.

It is all very exciting!

We can prove there is no "me" and "not-me" duality to our bodies in relation to the universe, but there is one underlying energy field. This field is responsible for our mind's highest functions—the information source that guides the growth of our bodies. It is our brain, our heart, and our memory. As Einstein put it: "The field is the only reality."

You, me, and everyone else on the planet start out the same. We are a creative energy.

You are not just a body. You are not just matter. You are

so much more! The you that is the most "you" is invisible, non-physical, and more marvelous than you might imagine.

If you remember science class, you know humans and all of our physical reality is made up of atoms. The atom is composed of electrons and a nucleus, which consists of protons and neutrons, right?

Atoms are extremely small. They are so small that accurately predicting their behavior using classic physics—as if they were tennis balls, for example—is not possible due to quantum effects.

So, if we are made up of atoms, what are atoms themselves made of? This is where it gets interesting because the truth is, they're nothing but energy vibrations!

An atom doesn't even exist as we know it until it is observed. If you remember the picture of an atom from science class, you will remember an image that looks like a solar system. This image is only partly accurate. Before an atom assumes that position, it is first in a state of unlimited possible variations. It is only when we look at it or try to measure it that everything "inside" the atom assumes a fixed orbit. Before that moment, it is nothing but a "probability cloud" of all the possible orbits it could be.

Yes! You read that right. What we are made up of, the base of all "matter," is a cloud of probability that doesn't resemble fixed matter until it is "observed" (or measured).

For those of you who want some science, here is a brief description of amazing research that will allow you to see a new reality:

British physicist Thomas Young conducted the famous "Double Slit" experiment in the early 1800s. In the experiment, he shot a light beam the width of a single photon at a wall with two slits in it. As you would expect, when one slit or the other was covered up, the electrons hit the wall after passing through the single slit and registered an imprint on the photographic plate. The pattern suggested the electron was behaving like a particle.

However, if both slits were uncovered, the single photon appeared to somehow split and go through both slits simultaneously. This created an interference pattern on the film that looked like white and then dark vertical lines. This pattern was similar to what you might expect when a series of waves are added together.

For example, imagine you are pointing a fire hose at a fence with two vertical gaps in it. If you hold the hose still, you will see two lines of water coming out through the gaps. However, if you wave the hose, some of the water collides and will cause a different result to come out the other side because it is a wave. All of this is relatively obvious, except when you learn what happens next.

When Young observed or measured the experiment, the photons behaved differently!

As the paths of the photons shot from the beam were measured or observed, the pattern exhibited a distribution on the photographic plate that would be expected from a particle. However, when no one was looking or measuring, it produced patterns that were wave-like.

So, the inescapable conclusion was that the act of observation caused the photons to behave differently than they did when no one was "watching" them. For this reason, Thomas Young stated, "The physical character of light was said to be observer-dependent."

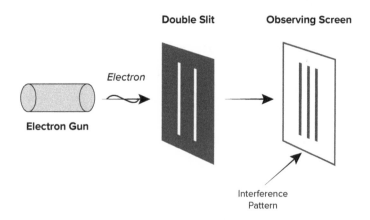

**Double Slit**    **Observing Screen**

*Electron*

**Electron Gun**

Interference
Pattern

In 1927, two American physicists, Davisson and Germer, expanded on Young's experiment and demonstrated that electrons showed the same behavior, which was later extended to atoms and molecules.

I hope you caught that!

The pattern and behavior of atoms—which you're made of—are dependent on conscious measurement or observation.

At the subatomic level, you are energy that exists in a "field of possibilities," and you will stay that way until the act of observation or measurement from consciousness "collapses" it from a wave of possibilities to a measurable "particle." It all depends on your ability to maintain focused attention.

Physicists at Princeton University and York University set up an experiment to find out if human consciousness could change how a light particle behaved.[1]

Participants were asked to observe light traveling through a Double Slit Experimental set-up with their mind's eye. The possibility of any physical contact with the set-up was eliminated.

---

1    Ibison, Michael, and Stanley Jeffers. "A Double Slit Diffraction Experiment to Investigate Claims of Consciousness-Related Anomalies." *Journal of Scientific Exploration* 12, no. 4 (1998): 543-50. https://doi.org/10.31275/08923310.

Researchers at Princeton University used subjects who had experience maintaining focused intention in these types of experiments. This experiment found that visualization had a small but statistically significant effect on collapsing the wave function. The York University experiment, which used a random group of subjects, did not find a significant effect.

In 2012, a team of parapsychologists, led by Dean Radin, conducted a group of six experiments on consciousness and collapse of the wave function.[2] These experiments found that the results depended heavily on the selection of the subjects. When experienced meditators were asked to see the path of quantum particles in their mind's eye, wave function collapse was slightly more likely. The results were statistically significant: odds against chance were 107,000:1. However, non-meditators were not effective in creating wave function collapse. Results of these studies, along with the earlier ones in 1998, were published in peer-reviewed physics journals. This is an interesting area of research, and hopefully, more experiments will be conducted on the issue.

What do these experiments show us? If, at a fundamental level, you are a field of unlimited possibilities or a stream

---

2    Radin, Dean, Leena Michel, Karla Galdamez, and Paul Wendland. "Consciousness and the Double-Slit Interfe ence Pattern: Six Experiments." *Physics Essays* 25, no. 1 (June 2012): 157–71. https://doi.org/10.4006/0836-1398-25.2.157.

of photons held together by consciousness observing, then you should be able to change the observation.

After all, aren't we the consciousness observing? If so, couldn't we simply change the observation of our base structure and change our complete reality?

The answer is yes; this is exactly what we see during a Superconscious Recode session. We connect to the essence of what we are and change the instructions (or observation); lucky for you, we have a shortcut that doesn't require years of meditating.

I've seen people go through Recoding and regain eyesight after decades of being blind. I've witnessed lifetime stutterers suddenly speak with confidence and diabetics who no longer need insulin. The transformations are amazing!

## BACK TO YOU: THE SELF-CONSCIOUS, UNCONSCIOUS, AND SUPERCONSCIOUS FIELDS

You are so much more than a body. You are an energetic charge that vibrates at a certain frequency in a unified field of information. You are a part of the uni-verse (one song) "looking back" at itself, experiencing a certain perspective or viewpoint. You are the field, and you are an individual perspective; you are both.

You are the wave of possibilities that has collapsed into a certain set of information (a body/identity/psyche) that now enjoys experiencing and interacting with other aspects/perspectives of the same field (other bodies).

You are the all, the one mind, and you are also unique. However, your unique perspective was created as an aspect of you, and then it created a set of instructions. If you are not enjoying your current perspective or experience, we can go back to those instructions and create a different code.

In my work, I have found many fields of information to be important; however, when it comes to understanding who we are, there are three classifications of energy that help to make sense of it.

These three classifications are your: Self-Conscious, Unconscious, and Superconscious fields. You may use different names, but here is how I classify the three:

1. The "Self-Conscious" (or Ego)—Defines itself through thought, an identity, a body, a name, and has a lifetime. Its goal is to live the best life possible.
2. The Unconscious (or Subconscious)—Defines itself through feelings, creates programs, and runs the body through automation. Its goal is to keep the system going, and its desire is to continue with what has been working (no matter how painful to the Self-Conscious).

3. The Superconscious—Defines itself as a code of information, has unlimited knowledge, and cannot think or feel. Its goal is to be involved in the creation.

The Unconscious is what guides all your decisions. Its number one goal is to keep you alive. If you are out of Unconscious alignment, you will not be able to take the action your Self-Conscious desires. This can be very frustrating. However, the Unconscious just runs on preprogrammed information given to it from the Superconscious. Let me explain.

Imagine a ship. The Self-Conscious is the captain, barking instructions. The Unconscious is the crew that makes things happen, keeps the ship running, follows instructions, and continues to build the ship. The Superconscious is what the Unconscious has available to use—the information, tools, ingredients, material, and knowledge. The Unconscious can only use what it is given from the Superconscious.

The Superconscious has an unlimited amount of information. It can access any information needed (remember the probability cloud); it is like the Genie from Aladdin and can change the information in a heartbeat. This means that when you can connect to the Superconscious, you can create whatever vessel you desire, travel to any destination, add or take away certain aspects/tools, or even change the ship completely (the Superconscious is the real key).

Many times, the captain barks instructions, is annoyed the crew is not listening, and the crew shouts back because what the captain wants is not possible on the ship!

This is why you must learn to connect to your Superconscious.

Every organic structure—including plants, the earth, and you—has a Superconscious memory. There is a Superconscious information code for each family, species, and society. The Superconscious is the unwritten information guiding us; it is always there.

The Superconscious is a field connecting all who are in a certain structure. This is why you see fish and birds flying in unison and migrating to the same place each year. This is why they arrive in this world in their perfect form, with preset fears and behaviors. This is how multiple people can get the same idea for an invention at the same time, and how a genius gets their inspiration.

The Superconscious is obvious in nature. We see the memory of information creating the same patterns, like the Fibonacci Sequence or the Golden Ratio. However, it is not a spirit or god; it is a unique information memory field designed to help each structure live its fullest expression.

The Superconscious has a unique memory for each structure, species, family, and individual. In humans, it has been observed that a memory (or traumatic emotion) can originate from at least seven generations in the past. This is so we do not have to "relearn" what can cause pain.

However, the memory can work negatively, as well. A client I recently worked with couldn't hold on to money, no matter how hard she tried. Therapy didn't help, and she was always broke. After accessing her Superconscious, we found a memory/instruction from her grandmother who, because of being rich, was targeted in WWII, and her entire family was killed. The memory's message was "money is dangerous."

No wonder my client had such a problem with money!!

If you want to live your true, fullest expression in life, you must have a working relationship with your Superconscious. Only when you do, can you finally witness the coding for your fullest expression and Recode the current information to allow much more satisfaction in life.

You can connect to the Superconscious of any structure, and with its permission, you can change the instructions, memory, or coding it delivers to that entity. When you change the Superconscious instructions that are given to a person's Unconscious, a new reality is possible. It will bring new results and brand-new behaviors. Imagine adding a motor to a boat or removing an anchor—both make a big difference. Without any pain or struggle, this change can happen in an instant, as you will see when you go through the exercises in this book.

## TWO ROLES OF THE SUPERCONSCIOUS

At our highest level, we are a "Superconscious awareness" and have access to all the information in the probability cloud. The information available consists of genetic, familial, species, historical, and planetary information.

The Superconscious is the aspect of you that can connect to this information and has two main roles: instructions and insight.

The first role of the Superconscious gives your Unconscious instructions on what to do. The Superconscious is the part of you that was there before you were a body, and it decided what information was important based on a memory structure downloaded from your family, species, and the world. These instructions are easily visible in the behaviors or results in your life.

When you connect to the Superconscious and "Recode" the instructions, you create new possibilities for your life. This is because the Unconscious aspect of you drives your life.

The Unconscious field of information consists of the feelings, body systems, traits, fears, genius, and health you are allowed to experience. The Unconscious takes the information it is given and reproduces it. The only goal of the Unconscious is to create the vessel (body) and keep it alive.

Again, you are an energy force and an observer. Your Superconscious takes all the possible information in the "probability cloud," also known as the unified field, and collapses it into matter, which is what manifests in this reality.

The Superconscious can access all information in the unified field of all possibilities and decides the instructions to give to the Unconscious field.

The second role of the Superconscious is insight, which is the ability to connect to an inner vision of the future or past, or to understand the instructions given to another individual. This ability to gain insight from the field and then turn the ideas into reality is how we create a life we love, access our genius intuition, invent new ideas, and plan for the future.

The problem is, most of us have never been taught how to predictably connect to the field, become Superconscious, and get this insight. However, all humans have this ability. In fact, there's nothing we have that wasn't first created in our minds!

You have the ability to become Superconscious and connect to the unified field of information. You can "see" what needs to be created in the future. You can access what is needed for other people, and you can even connect to the same information as another.

When myself or one of my coaches does the Superconscious work, a client will work with a coach. The coach "accesses" their field to help with creating new instructions. Everyone has this insight or ability to tune into the field structure of someone else. It is easily witnessed in puzzling occurrences of "simultaneous invention" or "multiple discovery," when two or more people have the same idea or discovery at the same time without knowing each other. A quick search on Wikipedia provides us with the following description:

> When Nobel laureates are announced annually—especially in physics, chemistry, physiology, medicine, and economics—increasingly, in the given field, rather than just a single laureate, there are two, or the maximally permissible three, who often have independently made the same discovery. Historians and sociologists have remarked on the occurrence of "multiple independent discovery" in science. Robert K. Merton defined such "multiples" as instances in which similar discoveries are made by scientists working independently of each other. As Merton said, "Sometimes the discoveries are simultaneous or almost so; sometimes a scientist will

make a new discovery which, unknown to him, somebody else made years before."

Commonly cited examples of multiple independent discovery are the 17th-century independent formulation of calculus by Isaac Newton, Gottfried Wilhelm Leibniz and others, described by A. Rupert Hall; the 18th-century discovery of oxygen by Carl Wilhelm Scheele, Joseph Priestley, Antoine Lavoisier and others and the theory of evolution of species, independently advanced in the 19th century by Charles Darwin and Alfred Russel Wallace. What holds true for discoveries also goes for inventions. Examples are the blast furnace (invented independently in China, Europe and Africa), the crossbow (invented independently in China, Greece, Africa, northern Canada, and the Baltic countries), and magnetism (discovered independently in Greece, China, and India).

Multiple independent discovery is not limited to only a few historic instances involving giants of scientific research. Merton believed it is multiple discoveries, rather than unique ones, that represent the common pattern in science.

## FIELD OF POSSIBILITIES

This infinite field of possibilities is there for all of us and can be used in many ways, which we will discuss in this book. You can use it to turn life into a wonderful creation instead of a struggle. Along the way, you will regain access to what you really are.

Once you have mastered the Superconscious code, you can connect to your Superconscious to change the instructions that cause limitations, disease, or frustration, and you can access the unified field of information to gain insight into the future, help others, and access your genius gifts.

When you remember who you really are and reconnect back to the Superconscious awareness, life will be so much more enjoyable, fun, easy, and playful. You are not just your Self-Conscious Ego. You are not your feelings or thoughts. You are much more. You are a creative energy. You are a consciousness that has "observed" or decided your way into existence.

So, are you ready to become Superconscious? Are you ready to let go of old beliefs that you are a body, separate from the world, and regain your connection to your Superconscious awareness?

Yes?

Great!

In the next chapter, we will discuss the individuation process so you can understand how you have forgotten who you are, and why forgetting was necessary. You will learn to "know thyself" and understand why most of us have followed a predictable path. You will learn what to avoid and identify the old patterns that pull you out of your truth.

## CHAPTER 2 REVIEW

At a fundamental level, you are a field of unlimited possibilities or a stream of photons held together by consciousness observing. You should be able to change the observation!

You are so much more than a body.

You are the all, the one mind, and you are also unique. However, your unique perspective was created as an aspect of you that created a set of instructions. If you are not enjoying your current perspective or experience, you can go back to those instructions and create a different code.

The three different classifications of consciousness are: your Superconscious, Unconscious, and Self-Conscious.

At our highest level, we are a "Superconscious awareness" and have access to all the information in the probability cloud.

The Superconscious can access all information in the unified field of all possibilities and decide the instructions to give to the Unconscious field.

# CHAPTER 3

―――·◆·―――

# INDIVIDUATION

When you collapsed from all possibilities into your human form, you had to forget that you were infinite possibilities and decide you were only separate. You decided to create a limited perspective of what was possible so you could experience the world.

Forgetting was the only way, because if you are everything, you cannot experience anything. The only way to experience hot is to know cold. If you are both hot and cold, you cannot experience temperature at all. So, you decided to create a limited view in order to feel, to experience, and to know yourself.

This is called *individuation*. It is the process of realizing you are a limited perspective in the universe. You created this experience because it was needed.

This limited viewpoint is human. You are just one perspective, one decision, and one point of the unified field experiencing a certain set of conditions and circumstances. You were given a name, you created a body, and you came into this world as an individual.

As an individual, you can experience more. You can experience contrast and make decisions about what you prefer to have. You created an idea of what the "perfect life" would be, what success meant, and a set of rules to avoid what you did not desire. However, these rules and decisions ended up becoming a prison you could not escape.

You came into the world vulnerable and powerless, needing a mother and father to feed you, care for you, love you, and validate you. However, in this creation of becoming a limited individual and giving over your power, you also gave others the ability to increase your satisfaction and cause you pain. Because of your desire to increase satisfaction and decrease pain, you created Unconscious rules to follow as you set out to figure out "how it is."

For example, you got yelled at for speaking out and lost dad's approval, so you created a rule not to speak out again. If you received praise for working hard, you continued to do that. If you received nothing for your hard work, you created a different decision.

For the first four to seven years of life, we go through huge Unconscious development: learning to walk, speak, and do everything else. The main goal of the Unconscious is to preserve the body and understand "how things are" so we avoid danger.

As an Unconscious child, we desire to know "how it is" to create more of what we love. If we don't know how it is, we cannot succeed. Therefore, we are always looking to create a narrative or find reasons why things are the way they are.

This is the basis of learning. We desire to avoid pain and experience pleasure. Pain registers five times more powerfully in the body, and so anytime we experience pain, it is crucial to find out why.

## ASKING WHY

Through the individuation experience, we learn we don't just have it all. We realize there is a way to have what feels good, and we know what feels bad, so we want to figure out why.

We always ask, "Why?"

If you are a parent, you have heard the question, "Why?" a lot, so you know exactly how important this is to every child.

We want to know why, why, why...WHY?

We ask, "Why" to avoid pain and have more pleasure. This makes sense, right?

Mum leaves me crying... "There must be a reason why."

Parents are fighting... "There must be a reason why."

We don't have enough food... "There must be a reason why."

Dad is yelling at me... "There must be a reason why."

I am being ignored... "There must be a reason why."

I get praise for being quiet/doing my schoolwork... "There must be a reason why."

I get told off for _____... "There must be a reason why."

I get abused/adopted/sent to doctors... "There must be a reason why."

Whenever we dislike something that happens to us, we look for rationality because we seek to understand the world.

There must be a reason why we don't get what we desire or a reason why we get it. Looking for an answer, we make a decision. This decision shapes the rest of our lives. It becomes the founding orientation of your worldview, and your life becomes about solving the answer to the question, "Why?"

This decision eases the pain we feel because now we think we know how to avoid the pain. This decision becomes a belief, and at our deepest level, becomes our orientation to the world. It can "sound" like:

"If I could just _____ then I will get/have/be/avoid _____."

"If I _____ then I am a good boy/girl. I will make mum happy, and she will stop being sad."

"If I _____ then I am a good boy/girl. I will make mum happy, and she will notice me."

"If I _____ then I am a good boy/girl, and I will make dad proud."

"If I _____ then I am a good boy/girl. Then dad will stop shouting, and we can all be happy."

The rules set up by our Unconscious to avoid pain end up defining us. They create our worldview and our identity. The problem is, we end up chasing solutions to solve this pain our whole life. Remember, we are never allowed to solve the problem because if we do, we will not know who we are.

This is the foundation of the problem-orientation that causes so much pain. Instead of going for what you want, you are trying to resolve an Unconscious rule structure from childhood. You forget what you really are and get consumed with solving this unbeatable condition.

After working with thousands of people and "digging" into what we really believe, I've found that most of us, at some point in our lives, made a fundamental decision that there was something wrong with us that we needed to fix.

We believe we are incomplete or missing something.

This decision is present because the Unconscious takes everything personally. Consider a child who feels pain but is ignored by their parent. Rather than rationalizing that it is because the parent had a busy day, the child assumes there must be something wrong with them.

This negative belief is so painful, it becomes the one thing this individual must avoid.

## SIX UNWANTED BELIEFS

I have found there are six unwanted beliefs at the foundation of the individuation phase.

1. I am not good enough.
2. I am not worthy.
3. I don't belong.
4. I am not perfect.
5. I am not capable.
6. I am not significant.

These beliefs are present in most people and are created through the process of becoming a limited individual. By taking on these beliefs, we forget we are an unlimited creative energy. In the attempt to overcome the beliefs, our identity gets caught in them and can never truly escape.

For example:

We don't have dad's love automatically, so we create a belief we are not good enough and must do something to BE ENOUGH. We have to prove we are enough. Our focus in life turns to finally proving we are enough. At the same time, our identity becomes that of a "not enough" person. Therefore, we can never have anything that would allow us to be enough because then our identity would have to die (and identities don't like dying).

Again, this is the biggest oscillating pattern in people's lives. They simply have an identity conflict that goes back and forth like a pendulum.

They can never solve the negative belief about themselves, and they can never truly be not good enough, because that is far too painful. So, they live somewhere in the middle: never being fully not good enough or good enough.

Each one of these orientating negative beliefs creates the same pattern, and this pattern is why people struggle to have what they desire.

## WHAT WE ACTUALLY DESIRE

The identity conflict is a big problem. Usually, the ideal life we've decided on is in stark contrast to the belief about what we do not wish to experience.

At the identity/Unconscious level, we don't actually desire what we are going for. We actually desire to overcome the negative belief we have about ourselves.

This is why someone strives to make a big impact in the world—to be deemed worthy; but they never create the impact they aspire to because, if they did, they would have to accept their worth.

Or why the person who is always looking for love rejects others before they get rejected, so they can always belong.

Or why a person continues to add more education or training to the list in order to be ultimately accomplished.

Or why someone desperately wants to create a business, but will never start because they must fix themselves and become perfect first.

The list goes on and on.

People don't actually go for what they want. They go after things they reckon would solve the negative belief that they created about themselves during childhood. The focus on overcoming the belief creates their structure and their reality.

This orientation is everywhere, and it has created a society and world of people who aren't living a life they love. They are living a life focused only on solving problems. A life without problems is not necessarily a life you love. Many only base their life on a focus of removing what they dislike, which leaves a numb, emotionless experience. A numb, emotionless, problem-less life is not a life full of joy and wonder and passion. The focus on removing or avoiding doesn't create this; it creates an empty life—this a big problem for people They are victims of their circumstances and conditions, and they have given all their power away.

The belief also creates a lot of fear. They will never allow certain things because they worry people would finally know the truth.

Again, they give all the power away.

Here is how some of the core beliefs show up in people:

I am not good enough, so I will never be satisfied with what I have. I will strive to be enough, yet I will never arrive.

"I am not worthy, so I will do things to prove my value and hope what I want will be given to me. However, I will never feel valued enough to succeed.

I don't belong, so I will build a big tribe/family to belong to and reject/judge others before they reject me. However, I will never fully feel accepted.

I am not perfect, so I will study hard, read every book, and be ready. That way, I'll never make a mistake. However, I will never start.

I am not capable, so I will collect resources, certifications, training, and money in an attempt to overcome my incapability. However, I will never have enough to do what I desire.

I am not significant, so I will desire to gain status, clout, uniqueness, and to finally be seen. However, I never will because I am not significant enough. No one sees me.

The underlying statement that could summarize all of these is: "There is something wrong with me that I must resolve to finally have the life I love."

In summary, we have forgotten we are a creative spirit. We are only attached to the limitation, not knowing that we created the limitation as a game, so we may experience this lifetime. We've forgotten we are powerful and can change the instructions we coded from our Unconscious in our effort to understand how the world is.

We all have a yearning or desire to become whole again and complete ourselves. This is motivated by a belief that we are incomplete or limited.

This individuation process was needed. We desired to become an individual and be one perception of the unified field; however, it is now time to experience both. It's time to become the observer and the observed, and to shift into a new reality where you no longer try to solve the misguided notion you are a powerless creator or a victim to circumstances.

You are the powerful energy that created it all!

### MY JOURNEY WITH INDIVIDUATION

As a young boy, my father played sports with me, and that was everything in life. I wanted nothing more than to be a professional rugby player because I heard how my father admired the players, and I saw the excitement on his face when he took me to a live game.

For me, success meant only one thing: being a professional rugby player. Growing up in New Zealand with the mythical All Blacks towering over you, it was the only logical choice. To be successful was to be an All Black.

I dreamed of the day I would make it on the team. I practiced the Haka in the mirror and knew this would be my future.

My first years in life were influenced by rugby. I took a ball to school every day. I'd arrive early to play before lunch, and then I'd go straight to practice after school. In my small world, I was the best. Then at about age seven, I moved away from the classmates I had grown up with and moved a year ahead to be with the senior students.

In this new class, the teacher had us run a circuit every day (probably to burn off all the extra energy seven-year-olds have). Every day, I turned up ready to win, and every day I was disappointed. The highest place I ever got was sixth, which was a horrible place to finish, considering most of the class couldn't care less and just walked. I didn't understand why.

One day, as I finished the race, I was mocked for my "weird running style." All the other kids thought the way I ran was hilarious. I was devastated.

One day while holding back tears, I told my father about this, and he confirmed my biggest fear. I was slow—really slow—and not at all athletic. Apparently, as a child, I didn't crawl. I had underdeveloped leg muscles, and my parents had taken me to all sorts of doctors. I was so upset that my dreams were being ripped away from me. All my heroes were athletic men who were admired for their physical attributes. There was no way I was making the All Blacks if I didn't change.

I decided I needed to fix myself. I urged my father to help "make me right." We tried everything: consulting sports physiologists who worked on national teams, personal trainers and coaches, training daily, and buying the most expensive shoes. We spared no effort to make me right.

This became my obsession, and my dad went right along

with it because he had the same structure. As a child, he was in leg braces and spent most of his youth swimming and weight training his way to achieve the dream of sporting success. Like father, like son.

We had our sporting successes, but not in rugby. At age fifteen, I played basketball for my country, represented my city in the under-20s, and was on the starting team that won the national title. We made it, and then I gave it all away. I stopped.

This pattern continued my whole life. I sensed I was broken and obsessively fixed myself to reach a goal, only to stop as soon as it was achieved and start all over again. It was like I was addicted to the chase.

When I looked around at others, I saw I wasn't alone. All of us are addicted to our patterns of needing to fix our reality or problem-solve to create an "ideal future," and we never get there. Our identity never lets us.

Do you see how the identity that creates the action/desire is in direct conflict with the desired reality?

## UNLEARNING THE LIE

The personal development world thrives from the idea that you must fix yourself. It keeps people in oscillating patterns. The truth is, you can have everything you desire right now. You do not need to fix yourself. Creating beautiful, amazing results has nothing to do with you as a person. Success is not personal. The idea that it is personal is a big problem.

Once I learned this simple and profound concept, I realized my dream life. I now run two multimillion-dollar companies (one earning nearly $1 million per month) from my home office in the paradise of the Gold Coast in Australia. I am married to the most beautiful, amazing, heart-centered, intelligent woman I have ever met (and yes, I am biased). I have great friends, play tennis every day, and lead a world-changing movement of people. It really is a dream come true.

Because of my experience, I'm passionate about teaching others how to create amazing results and a life they love in the fastest, easiest, most straightforward way.

When you become Superconscious, you simply learn to Recode the resistance that's in the way and take obvious action to turn your thoughts into things. Life becomes easy.

There is a lot of misguided information out there, so it will take some unlearning and relearning, but there is a process, and it is not what you have been told. Once you master this process, your life will be magic, because you are magic.

Consider all the things taking place in your body and around you.

You are the universe.

You are the creator.

This is us, and we are magic!

The decisions we make in the individuation process are needed, but they are literally childish. As a child, you had to do what your parents wished. You didn't have much choice as you were trying to figure out the world and make sense of it. You did your best.

Now, as an adult, you have the ability to create what you desire.

You can reconnect to everything that you are and change any instructions that are not serving you.

You do not need to know when, where, or why you have that code or those instructions in your field. You simply need to know whether it is working for you or not. If it isn't, you can Recode it!

The problem in our society is that we have no formal initiation into adulthood, so most people live the predictable path of oscillation and frustration. This leads to not being able to create what they love. Most think they can finally fix themselves enough to have success, yet that is the exact reason why they stay stuck.

In the next chapter, we will discuss the idea of structure and how it pulls things into reality. If the Superconscious gives you the material to build the ship, the Unconscious builds, runs, and maintains the ship. The Self-Conscious is the captain, and the structure is the body of water the ship is in. It dictates what is possible.

## CHAPTER 3 REVIEW

Individuation is the process of realizing you are a limited perspective in the universe. You created this experience, and it was needed.

The Unconscious takes everything personally and looks for the reason for any pain. The Unconscious believes there must be a reason why we aren't getting what we desire, or a reason why we get what we desire. In looking for an answer, we make a decision. This decision shapes the rest of our lives. It becomes the founding orientation of our worldview, and our lives become about solving it.

Because of individuation, we set up a life of problem-solving. Instead of going for what we want, most of the time we are trying to resolve an Unconscious rule structure from childhood.

At the identity/Unconscious level, we don't actually desire what we are going for. We desire to finally overcome the negative belief we have about ourselves.

You can have everything you desire right now.

You do not need to fix yourself because there is no need.

Creating beautiful, amazing end results has nothing to do with you as a person.

Success is not personal.

You have the ability to change any instructions that aren't serving you. You do not need to know when, where, or why you have that code or those instructions in your field. You simply need to know whether or not it is working for you. And if it isn't, let's Recode it!

# CHAPTER 4

# STRUCTURE

If you are like me, you were born into a problem-orientated family and society. The current reality is not enough, and we are all focused on creating "something better." Every client I have ever worked with seems to have these unwritten rules: *the future will be better*, and *now is not enough*.

This perspective begins with the individuation process we discussed in the last chapter. If you really desire to create big end results, you need a whole new way of thinking. You need to learn how to live in a creative-orientated structure instead of a problem-orientation.

## WHAT IS STRUCTURE?

A structure is a term that refers to a single thing with parts, and these parts have an impact on each other. A structure can look like a body, a chair, a song, a building—anything with individual parts that work together.

Your life-building process is also a structure. This structure has four parts:

1. A current reality.
2. The desired reality.
3. An identity.
4. An action to take.

These are the parts no matter how you structure your life.

1. There are three types of structures: stuck, oscillating, and flowing. A stuck structure is like a fence post.
2. An oscillating structure is like a rocking chair.
3. A flowing structure is like a wheel.

These structures can all be made from the same material (wood and nails) but will move in different ways.

When it comes to creating end results you love, you will always have the same ingredients (parts). But when you structure them differently, you will see different results.

All structures are held together by a magical force called "tension," which pulls things into reality and creates the path of least resistance. Once you know how to use tension, your life will change.

Think of tension like the force that is created when you stretch a rubber band. Inside of any structure, you have a "structural tension." This is what creates movement or lack of movement. The tension is what holds all the parts together.

The tension between two or more parts desires to be in equilibrium. If it is not, the movement will occur until the tension is resolved—tension is the potential that creates action. You see tension in a pendulum, which eventually comes to rest in the middle (where there is no tension).

When you move it to one side, tension is created to swing in the opposite direction. When it completes its swing and moves through, the tension is reversed.

## Tensions to Move

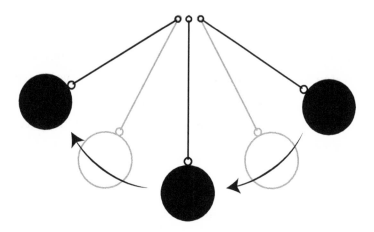

Think about your muscles and bones. If you increase the tension in your bicep, your arm bends. If you release the tension, it will straighten out again.

Have you heard the idea "the universe abhors a void" or "there is no such thing as a vacuum" (empty space) because the universe will conspire to fill it? These statements are other ways of describing tension.

Disequilibrium seeks equilibrium.

A void wishes to be filled.

Tension seeks resolution.

The law of tension is one of the most powerful laws in this universe.

The Superconscious creator must understand how to use creative tension to be pulled towards their end results, and to pull the end result to them.

How you structure your life makes all the difference because structure creates tension, and the tension creates the movement.

When you create tension in your life between what you have now and what you desire, you create a disequilibrium that needs to be resolved. The further you are away from the goal, the more tension you have. This is a good thing. It is the magical force that is about to pull you towards your goal. Tension seeks resolution.

The tension to move is increased by the distance/gap/ void between you and your desired goal. Remember that this desired goal is based on what you love, not on fixing a problem.

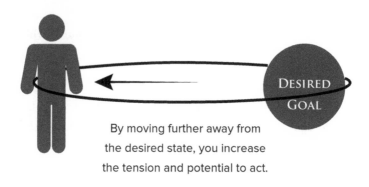

By moving further away from the desired state, you increase the tension and potential to act.

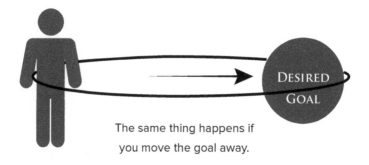

The same thing happens if you move the goal away.

Tension should seek a resolution and pull you towards your goal; however, you often don't reach the goal because you have created a competing tension.

The competing tension works against your true goal and creates the back-and-forth pattern in your life. This is called an oscillating structure.

### THE OSCILLATING STRUCTURE

To understand the oscillating structure, let's take a simple example of someone who wants to make more money. Because of their individuation process, they also have a competing belief that it's bad to have more than others. Therefore, as soon as they earn money, the tension is increased to give it all away.

By earning money, they decrease the tension of having no money, but they increase the psychological tension based around the idea that having money is bad. Once they give it away, they are back to having no money and desire to earn again.

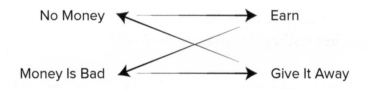

No matter the desire, the truth is the structure is not allowing the desired result to become manifested.

Many people have a current reality (CR) that is different from their desired reality (DR). They want to move towards their desire, but because their identity (ID) opposes the manifestation of the end result, they never create it.

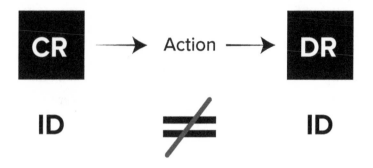

Because of this, many people have a life that is oscillating. For them, creating a life they love is like pushing water uphill.

As seen in the graphic, an oscillating life structure is created because of disequilibrium between the identity in the desired reality (DR) and current reality (CR).

Many overachievers structure their lives this way, and most don't know it. They think being motivated by the future is somehow better than not focusing on the negative. Many coaches make this pattern worse by having you associate how much "better the future will be" or by guiding you through the use of negative consequences. You can't trick yourself into action. You can only create competing structures in the unified field, and both will want to exist.

To understand the power of structure, you must understand the gravity of how we have been misled, and even lied to, by very well-intentioned people who don't know better.

## PROBLEM-SOLVING STRUCTURE VERSUS CREATIVE STRUCTURE

The difference between problem-solving and creating is huge. It is the difference between a lifetime of struggle and self-sabotage, or a lifetime of joyful creating.

Explaining the difference is easy; practical application is the difficult part. Structure is created where you put your original intention. If you put your focus on what you desire first and then take action towards it, you are in the creative-oriented structure.

If, on the other hand, you are sitting around thinking about what is wrong with you/your reality and then deciding you must go and solve that, your first intention is to solve a problem, not create. This is the problem-oriented structure.

The results from these structures are very different. By focusing on creating, you allow a flow or a pull towards what you want to create. By focusing on problem-solving, you oscillate and never get anywhere.

You can see the problem-orientation everywhere in our society, from the war on drugs to fighting cancer—everything is focused on the problem. The problem with focusing on the problem is that, as the creator, you are observing the problem into reality.

When you are solving a problem, you are taking action to

have something go away: the problem. When you are creating, you are taking action to have something come into being: the creation.

By observing the problem, you bring it into reality. You create a "point of observation" in the field that you then try to solve.

The problem-focused structure is inescapable. You will never solve the problem because the solution only exists in polarity to the problem. As you will learn in the book, structure has integrity and will create the end result it is designed to create. You must learn to be in the creative structure.

Let's do a small exercise. Think of something you do not wish to happen (for example, going broke or being ill).

Close your eyes and actively resist or try to avoid it happening. Notice how you feel. Notice what happens to the unwanted condition or circumstance.

Did it go away?

Likely not. It may even have become more powerful.

Now, let's try again.

This time when you close your eyes, accept the unwanted

outcome as a possibility among many possibilities. Simply accept that it could happen and acknowledge it. As soon as you accept it as a possibility, notice all the other possibilities that exist—some good, some bad. Notice them all.

How did you feel this time? What happened to the single possibility?

Likely it melted into a powerless position as you found your truth.

You see, what you resist will own you. As long as you are focused on resisting something, it will never go away!

Here's what's happening: when you resist something, you start by focusing on the problem. By doing this, you have collapsed the wave of possibilities into a "problem" you then decide to change. You are creating two separate "waves in the field," which causes all sorts of challenges. When you learn to focus on what you are creating, you will find a magnetism like you have never experienced, and you will witness miraculous transformation and results.

Again, the focus on trying to solve or fix unwanted circumstances/conditions/problems creates a lifetime of unsuccessful manifestation and total frustration.

To drive this point home, let's use health as an example.

Many people who are stuck in a loop of ill health do not realize they have created the experience. They blame themselves and think they are the reason. However, there is something bigger at play, and that is the structure or orientation to the creation of health.

Let's use a fictional story that may be familiar to you or people you love.

Let's imagine "Sarah" has a problem with being tired and bloated. She is also not sleeping well. She goes to her well-meaning naturopath, who asks her what the problem is and then decides she needs to do a food allergy test. The test comes back, and Sarah is put on a specific diet.

Her symptoms improve mildly but don't go away. After a while, she is back to where she started.

So, looking for another solution, she decides to go to an acupuncturist who asks her what the problem is, tests her pulse, and decides it is an energetic imbalance. She is told to come back weekly for three months, which she does.

Her symptoms improve mildly but don't go away. After a while, she is back to where she started.

Still frustrated with the problem, she decides to go to a kinesiologist who does tapping. This person asks what the problem is, and after some muscle tests, decides it is an emotional imbalance. The solution is a twelve-week program to become free of all negative emotions.

Her symptoms improve mildly but don't go away. After a while, she is back to where she started.

Years pass, and she tries more modalities, even going to a traditional doctor who labels it "fibromyalgia." Sarah has tried diets, fasting, meditating, frequency devices, supplements, exercises, colonics, therapy...you name it, she has tried it.

By this point, the number of people who have "observed the problem" is in the hundreds.

Now there is a field structure based around this illness. In fact, Sarah has a whole sub-personality or identity created to solve this problem (the only reason it exists is to fix the problem).

The more she tries to fix it, the more she stays the same. Short-term progress is quickly replaced by the symptoms, and her frustration leads to her just giving up.

Luckily, there is a better way.

Sarah has experienced the problem with problem-solving

(yes, it is ironic). Because she focused on the problem and simultaneously tried to solve it, she created competing intentions that must fight each other.

The first intention was to "find a problem," and the second intention was to find a solution to that problem. Can you see the conflict?

Sarah is in an Unconscious pattern with both the problem and the desire to solve it. Which one will win? Neither!

The only way for Sarah to move forward is to create, not problem-solve. The only way she can be in a creation orientation is to first become satisfied with her current condition, and to be happy with the now.

You must become happy now, even if the condition of the problem is still present. You must master the moment and "be in the end result."

Sarah can stop trying to problem-solve, accept that she is the creator of everything in her reality, connect to the part of her that is creating the unwanted conditions, and change the instructions.

Remember, your Unconscious is only following the instructions your Superconscious has given to it. You are a collapsed wave of possibilities showing up as "matter."

When you change the instructions, you will change the result.

It's easier than it sounds, and you have the guide in your hands. Stay with me.

## THE MYTH THAT IS STEALING YOUR DREAMS

A big myth we have been told is that to create success, we must have the perfect beliefs, be super-talented, or be lucky.

We have been told that success is personal (i.e., it is about you), there is a way you must be to create success, and there is a way you can be to create failure. This perspective denies the truth of what you are: a powerful creator who has access to everything.

So, let's examine the premise that success is personal. But first, let's define success. Success is the desired completion of a result you intended to create.

As a society, we have become addicted to an idea of success, and as individuals, we have decided what a successful life does and doesn't look like. Most people want: a happy relationship, healthy body, loving family, financial abundance, spiritual connection, great friends, time to do what they love, and the chance to make a difference. We all want very similar things.

The question then becomes, why don't we all have it?

Why isn't everyone a success?

It's obvious, right? Not everyone is talented enough? Maybe the ones who succeed are just "lucky," born in the right house, have a genetic advantage, or maybe it's something else.

As children, we didn't have the ability to create life the way we wanted it. We had it given to us by our parents. We had to live the way they prescribed. We ate what they ate, dressed in the clothes they bought for us, and went to the church they went to. At school, the teachers told us what we could or couldn't do, and we built beliefs according to what we were told.

The biggest belief is, "I can't have what I desire if I am the way I am." I need to improve, wait, study harder, be quiet, do what I am told, focus on other things, or sacrifice to get what I really want. All of us created a different belief based on one core childhood viewpoint: "I'm not able to have what I want the way I am."

Some of us decided we didn't have it in us to create what we love.

Some of us decided we needed to be a good boy/girl to have what we want.

Some of us decided there was something wrong within.

Some of us decided to reject everyone else because we felt rejected.

Whatever we decided, we all created a belief that we just aren't allowed and/or don't have the ability to create what we love for any reason other than loving it.

The world has been conditioning you to believe you are not where you need to be, and there is something you must fix to get there. We are fed everything you must be—sexy, or cool, or smart—by advertising and mass media projects.

Your teachers said you must be great at everything (which is impossible), or else a lifetime of failure would be the result.

But as Einstein put it, "If you judge a fish on its ability to climb a tree, it would grow up believing it was a failure."

This identity has become *you*. You have become powerless. You gave your power away as a child and decided outside influencers were needed to give you what you really desire. You needed to have a family to feel love, a relationship to feel good enough, money to feel you are safe, and/or a degree to feel you are competent. This identity seeks to find everything it desires *outside of itself.*

Many people are shocked to realize that many people they look up to, or those regarded as successful creators, did not have to fix themselves to create success. They didn't even have positive self-esteem or a perfect mindset.

Instead of being focused on themselves, they were focused on creating their result. They were connected to the unified field to master their craft. They focused on an end result even in the face of tremendous "failure," self-doubt, judgment, drug problems, and more.

There are past business icons, like Ray Kroc and Colonel Sanders, who, despite obvious personal flaws, were successful (even super late in life). Today, we see those like Elon Musk, Zuck, and Buffet all focus on creating their end result without fixing themselves.

In music, we've seen amazing creators like Michael Jackson, Kurt Cobain, and Amy Winehouse who didn't have perfect beliefs about themselves. They were all different personally, but they were similar in how they created big results. This is what I am interested in.

If you read the biographies of successful people, you will find that many of them were successful before the "self-esteem movement," and they reached their results without aiming to fix themselves or become perfect.

Many successful people didn't have "perfect beliefs." Instead, they focused on creating what they loved and followed through. Here are a few: Michael Jordan, Abraham Lincoln, Helen Keller, Beethoven, Steve Jobs, J.K. Rowling, Einstein, Hemingway, Churchill, Eleanor Roosevelt, Amelia Earhart, Edison, Elvis, Alfred Hitchcock, and Walt Disney.

Some of these people were not happy in life, and you may not like who they were as people. The point of using them as examples is to prove you can be a creator of amazing end results without the perfect belief system, being liked, or fixing yourself.

Luckily, you will later see the Superconscious Creator Code also allows you to create what you desire and feel happy about life along the way. This is because the Superconscious Creator Code is about how to create without fixing yourself.

History is full of people who arrive at success just the way they are. There is no right way to do anything (no matter how many times you've been told there is). You have a genius; you have a way to do life that is perfect for you. You do not need to fix yourself.

In summary: You can create anything you like, just the way

you are. This allows you to be free instead of trying to be something else or trying to fix yourself.

Instead of wasting energy obsessing about fixing yourself, you can focus all your energy on what it is you desire to create.

## THE TRUE COMMON DENOMINATOR

A statement I hear from many who are struggling is, "I have been trying to achieve _____ my whole life, and I can't. It's hopeless. It must be me."

They are saying, "In all my failure, I am the common denominator."

They make it personal. They decide the main reason for not succeeding is because there is something wrong with them, something they failed to do. So, they decide to fix that and make it right. They change their relationship, get a new business idea, or commit to a new diet. They decide to work harder, study more, or read another book. After years of this pattern, they simply give up and believe "it just wasn't meant to be." They just weren't meant to have that result. They give up.

However, if this was true—if it was all about the person—then why is it that nearly everyone around them is struggling with the same thing? If they really are so "terrible at success," then why aren't they the only one who is not successful?

See, there is a common denominator in all failure and in all success. It's structure.

The common denominator in all failure is the problem-oriented structure of "now is not good enough" or, said differently, "the future will be better."

This structure sets up a pattern of living for the future, and because you never practice being the person who has the future results (love, abundance, health), your core Ego/Self-Conscious identity can never accept them when they come into reality.

Because our current reality does not equal the desired reality, we can never keep it. If in our current reality, we feel unsatisfied, frustrated, living in scarcity, and not enough, we can never accept an opposite reality. To accept it would mean death to the way it has always been.

This structure is everywhere in society and is the number one reason people do not create a life they desire. They are in a never-ending oscillating structure.

| **Current Reality** | | **Desired Reality** |
|:---:|:---:|:---:|
|  |  |  |
| **Worse** | | **Better** |
| *Unsatisfied* | | *Satisfied* |
| *Frustrated* | | *Happy* |
| *Scarcity* | | *Abundance* |
| *Not Enough* | | *Enough* |

Identity will ***reject the future*** because to have it will mean *death of the way it has always been.*

This true common denominator—the structure of "the future will be better" and its unwritten shadow of "the now is not enough"—is everywhere in society!

Our countries are built on it, politicians claim it, and institutions indoctrinate us with it. The future will be better, they say, and we believe it.

But when?

When we have automobiles, go to the moon, or can stop polio, then it will be better...

Download this app, buy this new appliance, and work harder, then it will be better...

Get a higher education, save for a bigger house, or fight this war, then it will be better...

But was it ever better? Why do over 60 percent of marriages end in divorce? Why do 95 percent of businesses fail? Why is our health the worst it has ever been?

You are not the common denominator. This structure is!

## THE SABOTAGE LOOP

If you have lived in an identity of "not enough" for thirty, forty, fifty, or more years, it really doesn't want to change. So, it creates a sabotage loop. If this identity were to accept the future, it would have to give up all its patterns and effectively die.

For example, if you grew up a member of the working-class, like me, and had a scarcity mindset about money, you likely created a future that said, "When I am rich, I will feel abundant." Your identity became scarcity.

This is what you knew; therefore, as you get closer to the goal, the identity becomes more "worried" that it will die.

All of its safety has come from being who it is. Change is scary, so it does whatever it takes to stop you.

This opposing force is called resistance, and because you will always take the path of least resistance, it can stop you dead in your tracks. This loop is called "self-sabotage."

This resistant force comes in the shape of some thought pattern or feeling that communicates how "you don't have it in you to achieve the goal." This then motivates you to resolve the tension of the belief.

If you do not have it in you to achieve the goal, then you must act in alignment with this belief. So, you procrastinate, change ideas, overthink, enroll in a course, read a book, go to therapy, break up, change your diet, or do a million other things to stop yourself.

These distractions feel good because they are in line with your current identity and have no conflict. It feels good to pretend you don't know enough and enroll in more education instead of moving ahead and facing failure. But after feeling good for a while, you realize you still don't have what you desire, feel unsatisfied with your current reality, and start the process again.

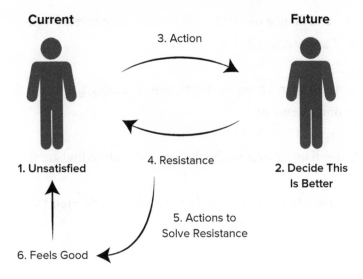

**Current**

3. Action

**Future**

1. Unsatisfied

4. Resistance

2. Decide This Is Better

5. Actions to Solve Resistance

6. Feels Good

The self-sabotage loop is like having a rubber band around your current experience in life/identity and another one around what you desire to create.

Moving in any direction creates more tension in the other path, and you will end up bouncing back and forth between the two realities.

Even if you use willpower alone to obtain the desired reality—the money, relationship, or fame—you won't allow yourself to feel or experience it. The now is still not enough, and the future will be better (the structure never changes), and you race off to another goal. This becomes life, and you never "get there."

You end up in a marriage still searching for love, or you go find a new one.

You end up in a business that is not big enough, or you quit to find a new one.

You end up solving one health problem only to find another.

We are addicted to self-sabotage. We are addicted to the structure of "not enough."

## ARE YOU IN THE PROBLEM-ORIENTATION?

You can have it all now and still create everything you desire, but most of us don't. Why? Because most of us are unknowingly in the problem-orientation. We are giving our power away to conditions and circumstances we want to avoid rather than focusing on what we desire.

A fast way to see what you are really focused on is to ask yourself, "What am I not allowing to exist, and what am I really avoiding?"

The conditions you will not allow to exist are blocking your desired end results.

What will you never allow to exist?

- Being broke?
- Being overwhelmed?
- Being called lazy?
- Being unhealthy?
- Being unsuccessful?
- Being single?
- Losing control?
- Being judged?
- Letting your family down?

It's interesting to ask, "What will I avoid at all costs? What is my Unconscious scared of being true about me?"

For me, it was being seen as lazy. I would avoid that at all costs. I could allow anything else for a short time, but I could never ever be called lazy.

This became a problem. I experienced burnout and was unable to take a rest. I started more projects, only to have them fail. "But at least you're not lazy." I could hear the voice of my past in my head.

The truth is, you are a prisoner to the condition you won't allow to exist—it literally owns you. The actions motivated by the beliefs are not yours; they are the actions of the identity that will not allow the condition.

This condition is viewed as death. It is not allowed.

What is the unwanted condition for you?

The great thing is that everything you want will come faster when you allow this condition to be possible.

My business grew faster when I was allowed to be lazy. When my clients allow themselves to have no resistance to any condition and still feel the same, they have mastered the moment and reach end results faster.

Here's the truth for you:

- If you allow failure, you will succeed more.
- If you're not worried about being broke, you can finally be rich.
- If you're allowed to feel overwhelmed, you will break through.
- If you're okay with being single, you can find the love you desire.
- If you can let go of control, you can find real safety.
- If you're allowed to disappoint your family, you can find yourself.

If you're still not convinced, go a step further. What would really happen if that unwanted condition existed? I mean, *really existed*. What would happen?

Maybe you would lose some friends or have to start again or get redirected to a new focus.

Maybe it would change everything.

But it will not change *you*, because you are not your results.

If you are worried about the existence of a certain condition, you have given it your power, and therefore you are in a powerless structure and will not create what you desire. You will only create more of what you want to avoid.

It is time for you to shift into a flowing structure that moves your current reality to your desired reality with ease. The key to creating a new structure is focus.

### THE FLOWING STRUCTURE

So, how do you move out of an oscillating or sabotage structure? You switch into a flowing structure. If you are flowing, the current reality and desired reality are not in opposition.

To do this, you must switch your focus and live the emotion of your end result now. You must be it before you see it. The flowing structure has no Identity (ID) resistance because the Identity is the same in either reality. You feel the same whether you have the success or not. You arrive at success and failure feeling the same. The feeling is the key, because that is the domain of the Identity.

You don't make your end result personal. You know the end result doesn't change you.

This dissolves the psychological tension, so there is no competing structure fighting for resolution. Once you do this, your end results will flow with ease.

This structure results in the path of least resistance being the correct action to close the gap. This is how you must have your life structured.

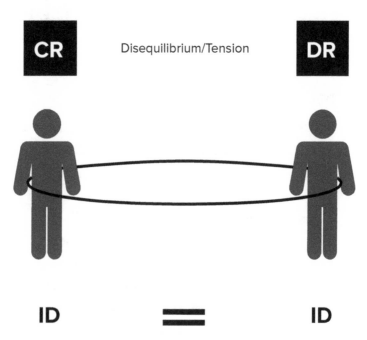

To shift into a flowing structure, you must shift your focus because your focus creates your structure, which creates your reality.

If you are focused on what you would truly love, you can have it and have it now. You will also be able to move toward more of what you would love to create with ease (this is what you will do in the next chapter).

If you are focused on avoiding, problem-solving, or fixing, you will self-sabotage and oscillate.

If you are in the wrong structure, don't waste your time and money trying to create a result. You will only find yourself moving in the exact way the structure allows, and nothing you can do will change that.

Here's a little example of how focus creates the structure, which in turn creates reality:

You decide life isn't good enough just having a job. You see others "living the entrepreneur dream," so you start a business. You want abundance and freedom, too.

Everything is going fine until one day you scroll on social media and get the idea that others are moving way faster than you. You look at your business and decide your business isn't growing fast enough, you don't have enough impact, or you aren't making enough money. (You've found a way to stay not good enough).

Your focus is now on taking action, and as soon as you do, you are met with self-doubt, imposter syndrome, fear of failure, the worry of judgment, and anxiety. These powerful emotions pull you. The psychological tension is strong, and you go looking for answers. You find many people ready to explain what's wrong with you. You are told, "If you believe, you can." You are told, "You must think rich to grow rich."

Your focus now is on fixing your beliefs. So off you go... hypnosis, NLP, EFT, the Law of Attraction, The Secret, meditation, Robbins' training, audiobooks, workshops, retreats, the emotion code, and all the rest (all amazing, but destructive when in the wrong structure).

You make some progress and feel good. Through this experience, you "realize" the business you are in just isn't right, so you start a different one. You are fired up and ready to start. A few months later, you find yourself paralyzed with self-doubt and fear again.

The cycle starts again.

In all of this, what was your true focus? Was it true you wanted abundance from the beginning? Or were you driven from a place of "I am not good enough."?

This focus on not being good enough is what started the structure, and anything you do inside of this structure only reinforces it.

So, after all of this, you can't give up the structure. The "I am not good enough structure" is still there.

You were the creative force that collapsed the wave of possibilities into that identity. You made it so.

You go after more knowledge to try and fix the problem. You learn a lot but don't achieve the results you want. You decide it's still not enough.

Or,

Your family looks at what you have spent to start the business, and they judge you. You decide you are not enough.

Or,

You make money but don't feel you've helped enough people. Why haven't you written that book already? You decide it's not good enough, so you set out again to create the life you want. But there it is again, that doubt.

Just one more course will fix it, right? WRONG. You will

keep oscillating or remain stuck because you are in the wrong structure with the wrong focus.

You can replace this example with love, health, family, spirituality, or anything related to your goals. You can replace "not good enough" with "not worthy, not capable, not significant, not perfect, or don't belong."

And you will get the same results.

The only way out is to focus on what you really love and to have it now. In a flowing structure, you are the same person in all circumstances.

Now you are aware of what structure is and why it is so important. It's now time for us to step into the creative orientation and start the Superconscious work. This is the turning point. This is the shift.

Before you step into creating end results you love, you must unlock the wizard's gate and have it all now. Otherwise, everything you do will only reinforce the old structure.

## CHAPTER 4 REVIEW

In the problem-orientation, we always want to "fix it" or make it better. This societal structure invades all aspects of your life, and because of it, you never create a life you love. Successful people do not focus on fixing themselves; they focus on creating.

You are not the common denominator. The structure is!

There are three types of structures: oscillating, stuck, and flowing.

If you change the structure, you will change the action and, therefore, change your results.

How you structure your life makes all the difference because the structure creates the tension, and the tension creates the movement.

With the correct structure, the tension will seek resolution and pull you towards your goal.

The key is not to make your end result personal and to know the end result won't change you. You can have everything now and choose to create what you love, but what you create does not change you.

When you have EVERYTHING now and still want to

create more of what you love, you are a Superconscious creator.

# CHAPTER 5

---

# THE MAGNETIC MOMENT

The NOW is the FUTURE when it comes to your identity, your emotions, and how you behave.

When there is no difference between your identity in the current reality and your desired reality, there is no resistance.

The way you feel now must be how you will feel in any future. If you want to manifest thoughts into reality fast, you must make this shift. When you do this, you are not dependent on a future outcome to feel a certain way. You arrive at success or failure as the same person.

You must be 100 percent satisfied with life now and desire to create more of what you love.

This is what I mean when I say you are "IT" ...always. Both satisfied and driven to create. Peaceful and powerful. In love with what you have and involved with what you are creating. Focused on the end result and loving the journey to get there.

By stepping into your future feeling and experiencing it now, you may be worried you will "lose motivation." If you already feel 100 percent good/abundant, why would you take action?

When your identity says, "If I had it all now, how would I be motivated to do anything?" it's showing its cards and letting you see just how much it rejects achievement of the end result. It's more worried about losing motivation than having what you believe you want to have.

You can have everything now and choose to create what you love because the everything you seek is not found in your creation. You are not your creation, and what you create does not change you.

You will be the same person whether you are a millionaire, broke, healthy, unhealthy, single, or in a relationship.

You can have it all now and choose what you would love to create; however, that desired reality is not better; it's just different. A different flavor of the same reality—not better, just different.

It's like you are completing a masterpiece painting. You have not changed. *The creation* has changed. When you are able to realize this, your results don't change you. You are free to have anything you choose. Just like going out to dinner and picking off a menu, ordering your end results from life should feel just the same.

You might say, "I will have a million dollars please, and a side of unconditional love." Great! Whether your creation is at the beginning, middle, or end of the journey, it won't change you. You are not it. You are separate from the creation.

When you really arrive here, now, complete, being everything, and with a desire to create what you love, you become a magnet for what you desire. There is no resistance to taking the correct action. We will cover this in more detail in the next chapter.

When you have EVERYTHING now and still want to create more of what you love, you are a Superconscious creator, and life is so much fun.

Could you be the same person, regardless of external circumstances?

Could you be happy now, independent of external circumstances?

Could you arrive at success and failure and feel the same emotionally?

Could you make success structural and not personal?

Of course, you can.

To do this, you must "be it before you see it." You must learn to "own the moment" 100 percent of the time.

I remember being told, "Chris, you will only see it when you be it," and I thought, great, so how do I do that? Then I was told not to fix myself, which seemed contradictory. How could that be possible? I have to be something else, but I can't fix or improve myself?

I saw a contradiction because I didn't know what I really was. I didn't know I was a creator, and that I had created everything. I didn't know I only needed to reconnect with the aspect of myself that was the Superconscious to re-create a new set of information.

Everything is always created twice—once in the invisible and then once in the visible, so there is no reason you can't have it now.

There is nothing you desire that you cannot have now, because everything you desire is already you. You are everything. Each desired reality, at its essence, is a feeling or frequency of emotion, and you have control over all of your feelings.

You have the ability to close your eyes and have it now. I have not met a human who cannot find some aspect of love, gratitude, abundance, and health now.

Now let's be clear, there are rules in the three-dimensional reality. Just because you are already "it" in the invisible doesn't mean it just turns up. We will discuss those rules later.

However, if you do not become "it" in the invisible, you will NEVER see it manifest in this reality. This is the first step, and without it, your identity will reject it.!

Let's consider three big outcomes most people want in their lives: financial abundance, long-lasting health, and romantic love.

No matter your situation in life, you have more abundance now than the richest person had one hundred years ago!

What you can access with free Wi-Fi at your local library is amazing. You have access to food you didn't have to grow at your local store. There is no reason you can't have financial abundance now, regardless of your bank statement.

Maybe you think you couldn't possibly have health now because of your "diagnosis."

The truth is, we are all in and out of good health all the time. The body is in total flux, and there are many parts of you that are healthy right now!

You can focus on the healthy things. That is actually what most "healthy" people do. They notice how good they feel. Everyone has places of disease; however, the chronically sick continually tell themselves how sick they are. The placebo effect shows that our bodies are built to heal and recover. And if you tell yourself you are sick, then you will be.

Your body is made to heal. You are the product of millions of cell divisions and millions of generations WHO ALL SURVIVED. You are built to survive. Your body is amazing! If you give it the right environment, anything is possible. Plus, if you're sitting and reading this right now, you can focus on how you *do* have health!

What about love?

You might be thinking there's no way to have this now because you're single.

Not true. Love is a verb. Whatever you want to receive, you must give. By giving it, you receive it. In truth, many who are in a relationship still don't feel love because they have not practiced giving love. You can be full and connected with anyone (including yourself) by giving love.

So yes, you can have it now... You can BE it before you see it.

This is a universal truth. What you plant will grow. You cannot plant seeds of scarcity and grow a forest of abundance.

If you were to break open a seed to find the instructions on how it would turn into a tree, you would not find it. However, the seed has all the instructions within it to become the perfect tree and forest, yet you cannot see those instructions. They are invisible. This is the same as you. You are planting your thoughts into this reality, even if we cannot see them.

Remember, everything is created twice: in the invisible and then in reality. It's all in the mind.

The seed IS the forest, and you ARE your end result, even if it hasn't manifested in this reality yet.

Nothing outside of you will give you what you really want. You must give it to yourself!

Once you change your orientation, everything will flow. Trust me; I fought this idea for a long time. I thought that by thinking the future would be better, I was doing it right. I thought I had to fix or improve myself. I gave my power away.

Once I learned to become whole now—to have it without seeing it—the momentum was huge.

I am the same guy, just in a different structure.

To help you understand how you and what you create are separate, let's take a look at money. Remember, the result doesn't require you to be a certain way, and therefore it won't change you. There is no identity conflict in true creation. You simply choose to have it.

## THE CREATIVE STRUCTURE OF MONEY

Everything you desire to create has a structure or set of rules for how it will come into existence—even money. I am grateful to be financially free and have more money than I can spend on my needs. It feels great, and it's not where I started in life. I had to learn about money the hard way.

I've had an interesting relationship with money. As a child, my biggest desire was to have the best sports equipment, shoes, bats, balls, you name it. I wanted to have the best, but I couldn't. I was told what was affordable and what wasn't.

Money was a scarce resource because I grew up in a working-class environment. My family and everyone I knew had to trade their time for money, and because time was a limited resource, so was money. There was always stress around it, and I had a desire for more.

While this desire was true for me, I didn't understand money or how to have what I desired. Money is not created by time, and even if you grew up in a "trade time for money" environment as an employee, you can change your orientation to money. You must first learn its structure.

I was committed to making lots of money, and throughout my young adult life, I made it and spent it, always ending up with more debt. This cycle continued until I figured out what money was and how it is structured. Now my companies earn around $1 million per month and are growing fast.

There is a lot of misinformation surrounding money and how it is created. Here are a few top myths we must debunk:

"You need to hustle and work hard."

Don't you know people who do that and don't make much?

"You can activate your money DNA from another dimension."

The only people who say this sell a course on how to do that.

"You need to be in this opportunity or learn this thing."

Yet, in each opportunity, there are winners and losers.

"Money is an energy. The more you give, the more you get."

Don't many give energy and get nothing back?

"Money isn't important."

Yet those same people give their lives every day to get it.

Here's the truth: Receiving money is predictable and is a structure. You simply must understand what money is, along with its structure.

So, let's examine money. What is it?

Money is a measurement! It's a measurement of value.

What is value? Value is an increase in satisfaction or a decrease in pain for another human.

So, if you want lots of money, all you must do is add value to another human. You make their life better—so much so that they want to pay you for it—and you receive money.

You don't need to be a good or bad person. Money doesn't care.

You don't need to work hard. Money doesn't care.

You don't need to activate money chakras or codes. Money doesn't care.

You don't need to be passionate or talented. Money doesn't care.

You don't need to be educated or know a certain thing. Money doesn't care.

Again, money is a function of adding value to other humans, so they want to pay you for that added value.

It is a measurement—just like a mile, kilogram, or a centimeter. It measures something (a desired value).

You don't need to do a money dance or write affirmations.

You don't need to be anything other than what you are.

Money doesn't care about you.

If you grew up in a working/middle-class family, you might have had similar thoughts as I did about money.

I learned you had to trade time for money, and you had to get a great education so you could charge a lot for your time. Because time is limited, money creation was also limited. Over time, I created beliefs about how money only flowed with "hard work." This belief seemed true, but it wasn't.

Money is as abundant as humans have desires and problems they want to solve.

Instead of trying to trade time for money, I needed a structure that would create money without limitation. Because money measures value, I needed a value creation system that worked without me giving my time.

Can you see why, without getting into the correct structure, motivation will not work? And can you see it doesn't matter how much you work on yourself if you're not in the right structure?

If you desire to create a huge flow of money, you must simply understand it:

You must find a way to add value (in a way that others will want to pay).

You must find a way to deliver that value to them (with little time).

You must find a way to distribute value (without time).

Once you realize money is a structure, it becomes much easier. It will not change you, and you don't need to change. You simply must be in the right structure!

Whenever I teach this, someone always asks, "Well, what about the lottery?" And the truth is, lottery winners are just lucky. Millions of people put their names forward to win, and one wins. Sure, someone might say they used a secret manifestation technique to win the lottery, but what about everyone else who wished for the same result? The winner's confirmation bias makes them believe they did something to win when it was just luck.

Others say, "What about those who steal or cheat or lie? How does that fit? The answer is that it doesn't. It's outside of the rule; it's an exception. And there are always exceptions to a rule.

I've used money as an example here, but the same truths apply for anything you desire to create. You must get into the right structure and remember it's not about you. You will be the same person with or without it.

## BECOME THE MAGNET

Being a magnet for what you desire is simple. You must have the identity (thoughts/feelings) that allow you to accept the reality you desire to create. When you are in the correct identity, you can take the correct action. Because of this, it may seem as though things are "attracted to you" when in reality, you are creating them. You must realize you will be the same in all realities; they will not change you.

As an example, let's take two different seeds, say a carrot and a strawberry seed. If you plant them in the same soil, with the same water, they will both create different outcomes (a carrot and a strawberry plant). They created the end result of what they are, and there was action needed to make it happen (watering, planting, fertilizing. etc.). Both seeds were a magnet for their fullest expression. However, if the seeds were just left in a jar, nothing would happen. You must have both. You must be the magnet for what you desire and take the action required to see it manifest in this reality.

To be a magnet for your creation, you must accept the identity that is allowed to receive and live the end result that you desire. You do this by becoming it now. The fastest way to do this is by living the four specific "choices" mentioned earlier, the ones I call the core orientational choices. These four choices shift you into the magnetic moment. We will use your Superconscious to make this shift fast. You must become it now.

Keep in mind that you are always a magnet. You can't turn that reality on and off. What you create in your reality is a direct reflection of your identity. I used to live an identity of "not good enough," trying to prove myself to the world. I remember this identity intimately. It created a life full of stress.

I had a gym, two hair salons, a digital marketing agency, a speaking business, and multiple education businesses. I had over fifty people on staff, and it was chaos. Money was coming in one end and going out the other. I was on a plane every week to another city to run events, and when I wasn't speaking, I spent my day putting out fires.

I thought this was what I wanted. On the outside, I looked like a huge success; however, I was burning out on the inside.

And one day, I broke down.

It was about 11 a.m. on a Tuesday, and I went for a walk down to the beach. Everything was coming at me, topping off all my stress. I just found out I needed to come up with about $20,000 for a family health emergency, and I owed big money to the tax office that would basically wipe out my profits. I had the money to fix it; that wasn't the major problem. The real problem was that I was unhappy. I had no idea what to do.

I stopped at a park bench to sit and collect my thoughts. It was a beautiful day, and the sun was shining. I could see the surfers out enjoying the Gold Coast waves, and I closed my eyes to consider my options.

About five minutes had passed when my thoughts were interrupted by two homeless-looking men who were bumbling along. They talked loudly and carried fishing rods, clearly having the time of their lives.

Just what I need, I thought.

Feeling frustrated that my quiet time was interrupted, I judged them for what they were wearing and what they were doing on a Tuesday: fishing.

What a waste of time, I thought, and they need to get jobs.

Unfortunately, they decided to stop near me and discuss their morning. This seemed to be their ritual, what they did every day. One of them described how sorry he felt for all the "pencil pushers stuck in an office." As I watched them laugh and enjoy the moment, I realized they knew something I did not.

They knew how to be happy.

I realized I was not living my truth of what I really loved. I was doing something else.

I thought I wanted to be a millionaire entrepreneur with loads of investments, speaking on international stages. I thought I wanted to be really busy, but I wasn't really happy.

Everything I did was what my identity/Self-Conscious Ego had decided I needed to do; to finally prove to the world I was good enough. None of it was what I loved.

It's a hard pill to swallow when you realize the life you are living is not what you intended.

If allowed to start from scratch, what would you change?

The biggest loss in life is the loss of time.

If you are not living your truth, it's time to change. Now!

As my mother used to say, "Rip the Band-Aid off." It may

hurt in the short term, but it's "better to get it over with and done now."

I decided I would rather make $5,000 a month, live in a rented apartment, and enjoy my life instead of making a few million and waste time trying to prove something.

I decided to love life now, no matter how much my Self-Conscious thought I was losing it.

I knew what was true for me.

So, I did it. I ripped the Band-Aid off, and it hurt.

Within three months, I sold the gym at a loss, gave away the hair salons, and closed a company. I stopped the marketing agency and just focused on what I loved. It took another six months before I was finally "free," living my true choice and not living to serve my identity. I decided to spend time with my family, play tennis every day, and read. I decided to enjoy my life.

This is why the four core choices are so important. Without them, there is no point in trying to create anything else. There are many who desire to stay in a reality where they need to solve their old negative beliefs instead of having it all now. To have it now and still desire to create what you love, will require you to overcome internal resistance, but it will be the most satisfying thing you ever do. When you live the core four choices, you can then move on to creating what you really love.

Once again, the four core choices that orient you to a new reality and ensure you are living fully satisfied now are:

### 1. I CHOOSE TO BE THE PREDOMINANT CREATIVE FORCE IN MY LIFE.

You choose to be powerful and in control. You choose to react in the ways you desire when you live as the predominant creative force. You are the one choosing all your thoughts, feelings, actions, beliefs, and focus. You are the predominant creative force, but not the only one.

### 2. I CHOOSE TO LOVE MY LIFE.

You love every moment of this journey called life. You acknowledge that you created it, and every current reality is just another step on the journey towards the next. No step is better, and you will love your life now.

### 3. I CHOOSE HEALTH AND VITALITY.

This choice brings you into creative power with your health and energy. You regain control of your body and are no longer in situations where you feel like your body is against you. You reconnect to the power within all of us to transform and create any body we love.

## 4. I CHOOSE TO LIVE MY TRUE NATURE AND PURPOSE.

This choice ensures you are living in alignment with your fullest expression—whether as a parent, sports player, artist, lover, or musician. This is why you are here.

A choice is something you manifest. It is not a goal, a wish, or a dream. Everyone can have these "four core choices" in any situation. There is no valid reason or excuse for not being able to live these four now.

We work on these four first because there is likely a lot of resistance to having them now. Loads of beliefs, emotions, memories, and instructions from the Self-Conscious and Unconscious are in the way. Until you are living these four, you are always in a problem-solving reality. This is the first step. This is how to re-create the correct structure.

Once I was allowed to live these four choices, I was in the creative orientation, and many of the goals I had set earlier came to fruition. Only this time, there was total ease and flow.

It was strange to witness that once I let go, let myself have it all now, and no longer needed the external to complete myself, all that I desired showed up. Even stranger was how fast it happened and how little the external results really mattered to me. This is the key to Superconscious creation.

## CONDITIONING THE UNCONSCIOUS MIND

Your Unconscious mind is the domain of feelings. If you do not feel in alignment with what you are creating, you will self-sabotage. The Unconscious does not know the difference between a thought about reality and a thought you create; it takes each as the same. To prove this point, think of an uncomfortable, scary, or embarrassing story. Close your eyes and remember it.

Did you feel it in your body?

We all know we can have thoughts that are not happening in reality and have our body respond as though it is happening now.

This is key to conditioning the Unconscious mind.

Because we can control what we are thinking, we can control what our Unconscious receives from us. If we spend enough time sending new instructions to the Unconscious, this will become its new point of orientation, and this will be your new identity.

Your Unconscious is designed to keep the body alive and

running. It has adapted the body to be in alignment with the internal environment and will change and adapt based on how you change that internal environment.

Consider this example: Mary grew up in a stressful family environment. As a two-year-old, she witnessed her parents fighting, and when she was three, they divorced. This created a thought pattern of pain/abandonment, which sent instructions to her body to create feelings of unworthiness. Certain cells adjusted themselves to create a feeling to warn against loving someone because if you love them and they leave you, it hurts! This feeling became hardwired into her biology, and her Unconscious decided this was how the world is.

Makes sense, right?

She has a warning sign from her body to warn against something that caused pain.

But what if she wants to go for a loving relationship?

As an adult, Mary cannot figure out why she can't hold a relationship. Every time she gets close to someone, she finds a way to sabotage it. Every time she finds a relationship and feels love, she no longer sends the instructions to her body that she is unworthy.

This results in her body thinking something is wrong. After

a lifetime of receiving certain instructions and living in a certain internal environment, her body cries out like a heroin addict for another hit of unworthiness.

We can observe this in the amazing field of epigenetics. As discussed by Bruce Lipton in his book *The Biology of Belief*, a cell works like a "miniature human being" and will adapt/change its function based on the environment it is in!

This is why stepping into the emotion of the end result is so important. By taking this step, the resistance to achieving the end becomes obvious (you feel it) e.g., as soon as you imagine walking out on stage for a public speech, you can feel a rush of anxiety. This is true for all end results and allows us to use this process to uncover and Recode what is in the way of achieving what we desire.

Mary can treat the belief of unworthiness and realize she was always worthy. Her parents were just adults who needed to live separately.

It had nothing to do with her.

When she changes these instructions and lives the emotion of the end results, her body will shift and adapt to the new feeling. Then, when the right relationship turns up, she can accept it.

This is not problem-solving. It is actively creating, and the emotion of the end result is very important to ensure we have total internal alignment with what we desire.

We do not want to get in an Unconscious relationship with that which we do not desire, so we need to experience the end result and next action as if we were doing it now and feeling really good about it.

This is where visualization and imagination come in. You must first step in and actively experience living the end result to create the feeling, send the right instructions, and collapse the wave into exactly what you desire.

Many have it the other way around. Using the wrong language structure, they say, "If I have _____ then I will feel _____."

"If I had a million dollars, I would feel freedom," or "If I had a supportive body, I would feel healthy."

They have pushed the feeling out to *after* they achieve something. Instead, you must get into the feeling and then live that feeling now. The feeling is the communication system of the Unconscious, and it is 100 percent necessary to live the feeling first to have no identity resistance with what you desire.

We can pre-program our Unconscious mind to be ready to

accept the end result we choose. We do this through powerful closed-eye visualizations and meditations to create a new reality, a new present moment. I love to break down the words "present moment" into "pre-sent moment"—a moment previously sent by our past condition to create the current moment. You can create a different pre-sent moment by changing the instructions.

This is taught in many other modalities. The big problem with many of these is they don't first address structure, and they try to conduct this process from the wrong structure.

I remember doing thousands of hours in meditation, applying The Secret and the Law of Attraction principles, and seeing no results. So please remember, you must be in the right structure before you create. It is also much faster when you have the Superconscious working for you (which you will witness by the end of the next chapter).

The magnetic moment is a moment of total presence, where you do not resist or desire anything to change. You are completely happy with the now. You are totally satisfied with the now, and you desire to create more of what you love.

When you access this moment, you open the "wizard's gate." You are able to re-join with your truth as a creative spirit and command reality. If you do not access this moment, you will struggle.

The magnetic moment is not something you achieve just once—it's a lifestyle. It's a way of being, where you are so happy, where you are so satisfied, and yet you have a desire to create what you love. The near contradiction inherent in that statement is not lost on me. It took me years to fully live without trying to solve problems, trying to complete myself, or thinking a future is better AND still be motivated to create what I love.

Lucky for you, we have a clear process to make it happen with the four specific choices, which allow you to live in the moment with total satisfaction.

## THE EMOTION OF THE END RESULT

Through visualization and meditation, you can condition your Unconscious to have the ability to accept and live the end result you desire. The process is very simple and uses open-ended questions to allow yourself to "be it."

Here is the process that will form step two of our overall five-step system. This is how you open the wizard's gate. In the next step, you'll learn how to receive wisdom from the Superconscious field on exactly what you need to do to bring the idea into reality.

This is a closed-eye process, so quickly read through the steps and then give it your best. Start with the first choice:

"I choose a life I love." Allow yourself to fully experience that being true and teach your body exactly how it will be in your new reality.

1. Connect to your heart and feel the moment. (Take a few breaths with your eyes closed.)
2. Choose the end result of living a life you love and feel what it is like to have now. Accept it as truth and build a full sensory experience of "living it."
1. Ask an open-ended question to expand into possibility: "What are all the possible ways I have this?"
2. Notice what comes to you and feel it.
3. Ask another open-ended question and feel it: "What would I love to create to feel this even more?"
4. Open your eyes.
5. Repeat this process with the other three orientation choices:

I choose the end result of being the predominant creative force in my life.

I choose the end result of having health and vitality.

I choose the end result of living my true nature and purpose.

Spend at least twelve minutes on this exercise (three per choice).

How did that feel? Can you notice how your body feels alive by those choices?

Using the emotion of your end result is vital from an epigenetic, structural, and intuitive perspective. Next, you will learn how to bring the Superconscious into this creation.

## CHAPTER 5 REVIEW

You and what you create are separate. End results don't change you.

Your first action is to reorient to the world with the core four choices. These four will have you in a creative structure and allow you to have it now. Next, you can follow the five steps of a Recode session and ultimately connect to the Superconscious to change its instructions and reach your end result.

Remember, this is not problem-solving. When you choose an end result, you are creating. You are not focusing on a problem; you are forward-focused. You can have health and vitality now and still choose to create more of what you would love.

To take the step from powerless to powerful, you must step into a creative structure and plant the seeds into the unified field you wish to manifest. Let go of all that is in opposition to being it now.

When you live the "core four choices," you unlock the wizard's gate and step into a place of no resistance or desire. From here, you can choose any future reality without the internal civil war stopping you.

The core choices that orient you to becoming a magnet for your future are:

1.  I choose to be the predominant creative force in my life.
2.  I choose to love my life.
3.  I choose health and vitality.
4.  I choose to live my true nature and purpose.

# CHAPTER 6

——◆——

# BECOMING SUPERCONSCIOUS

For most of my life, I was told that power was outside of me, so I was on a continual search to find the answer. If there was ever a challenge in my life (health, financial, emotional, spiritual, or relational), I assumed there was something wrong with me that I had to overcome. Once I realized I had the power to create, transform, and heal, everything was different.

Our power has been hidden from us and is even labeled incorrectly. It is common knowledge there is the "placebo effect," which can be increased or decreased. The more a patient believes in the process, the more it will work. This is true even to the point that a patient gets better results from a sugar pill than others who are given a real pill.

The placebo effect just disguises our own power to create transformation in our own bodies. It's not an effect! It's our natural ability.

When you connect back to your power and realize you are not your body but creative energy that is having a body experience, you really can create miracles. Let's get you connected to your Superconscious and restart your working relationship.

## CONNECTING WITH YOUR SUPERCONSCIOUS

Your Superconscious mind is an infinite field of information. It is always there. You have been able to work with it many times before because it *is* you. Up until now, you have not had a system to connect and communicate predictably with this part of yourself. Your Superconscious works in two ways: to give you instructions on how to be and provide insight into the future.

Your Superconscious is always communicating with you. Let's do a small exercise so you can realize this communication. It is true you actually have three "brains" in your physical body, all aspects of your Unconscious mind. They all send you messages. The three are your heart, your gut/stomach, and your head. They are all connected to the Superconscious field. Let's do a quick exercise to become aware of this.

Please don't skip ahead in this process. Take it one step at a time for the full benefit.

First, think of a moment when you made a mistake and got something wrong.

Once you have it, close your eyes and experience the moment again, like a movie playing in your head. Create a full sensory experience of this moment.

Notice where you feel the emotion in your body. What kind of emotion is it? Are there colors associated with it? Allow yourself to go into the moment and observe what is happening in your body.

Now write down a few notes (e.g., I felt a sinking feeling in my stomach, and it was very dull, falling to my feet).

Now that you have done that, remember a time you did something right—when you won, and everything worked out.

Once you have it, close your eyes and experience the moment again, like a movie playing in your head. Create a full sensory experience of this moment.

Notice where in your body you feel the emotion. What kind of emotion is it? Are there colors associated with it? Allow yourself to go into the moment and observe what is happening in your body.

Now write down a few notes (e.g., I felt expansion in my chest and a tingling of energy that was light and free).

What is the difference between those sensations in your body?

Lots, I would assume!

Usually, our heart/chest field is activated when you are in your truth, growth, and positive end results. Your gut/stomach field is activated when you are coming from fear/uncertainty/doubt. You can learn how to get clear messages in this way, but for now, this general description is enough.

This is your first step to understanding you have many other communication systems besides just your "head brain."

I have become so fluent in how my Superconscious communicates with my Unconscious that I can get a read on nearly every situation instantly, without needing justification from my logical brain as to why it is right. This can take some time, so for now, we will focus on a three-step system for you to create a connection with your Superconscious.

To connect to your Superconscious, you must get out of your

thinking mind and go back into an innocent/open/present state where you are able to perceive what is happening without the judgment you have conditioned over your lifetime.

Our process of communicating with the Superconscious looks like this:

1. Go into innocence/drop into your heart.
2. Connect with the Superconscious through direct communication.
3. Get information through a message/symbol.

Let's explore each step of this process. To drop down into your heart or access innocence is to stop needing to know. The heart field is your connection to your childlike, playful imagination, which is the unified field. Most of us are not familiar with experiencing the world from this place. We stopped doing it a long time ago.

Remember, to make sense of the world, our brains create shortcuts to know "how it is." The shortcuts that we create allow us to navigate this world without having to re-learn how it all works.

When you see a baby at the beach for the first time, a kitten playing with a leaf in the wind, or lovers in the budding stage of romance, you can see the joy that comes from witnessing something for the first time.

Eyes wide open, fully present in the moment.

Unfortunately, you won't notice this on the face of many adults because they have already learned everything they need to know. They have generalized the world around them to fit into pre-programmed models that already exist, and they are missing out on accessing their Superconscious.

If it is not new or important, the brain does not want to take up extra resources paying attention to it. The first kiss eventually turns into a daily peck on the cheek. A once astounding sunset eventually becomes just another sunset.

By the age of thirty-five, you have likely witnessed most things for the first time, and instead of experiencing awe, most of your life is now aligned with the preprogrammed worldview of "how it is."

The truth is, so much more is going on than you are aware of.

If you have ever had a life-threatening experience, you have likely had an experience of Superconscious awareness. You were able to slow down time, give things more consideration, and make decisions at lightning speed.

This level of consciousness is always there, but you can't live there all the time. You don't need to re-learn what a truck is every day or become awestruck when a leaf moves. This would be exhausting. However, there are times when you want to be able to suspend what you think you know and go into a Superconscious awareness to get all the information.

In short, we are accustomed to Unconsciously deciding how something is. We do not give ourselves time to witness all that *really* is. The reality you think you see is actually not the reality that is there. You are making the reality fit your worldview of what is reasonable.

Your preconditioned patterns that control the narrative are also known as *confirmation bias*. We assume how something is supposed to be and find ways to prove our reality to be true, but you can basically prove anything! If you look hard enough, you can find a way to confirm any thought pattern.

You can confirm that men are liars and cheats. Yet, all the same, you can confirm they are great citizens. You can confirm the government is against you, and you can confirm they have your best interests at heart.

You can confirm all sides of any belief system, but in doing so, you don't truly recognize what is there.

To really see the truth, you must learn to stop needing to "know how it is." You must not know. You must go into a childlike place of presence, awe, openness, and innocence.

Only from this place can you see what is really in front of you, what actions you should take, and what is true. This is easier said than done. In a world addicted to the demand of knowing how everything is, we don't give ourselves space to really see things for the first time or witness them as they really are.

To move into a place of not needing to know, we must become innocent to the moment. This is the first step in hearing/perceiving what information the Superconscious has for you. Genius information and intuition are outside of what you already know.

The second and third steps involve connecting to the Superconscious to get information. There are two ways I communicate with the Superconscious: through direct communication and by receiving information I have to decipher.

Direct communication with the Superconscious is easy to do and is done most effectively with muscle/body testing. Body testing is a good way to get answers straight from your Superconscious because it goes around your thinking brain. I have coached thousands on this method, and they get a yes/no answer from the Superconscious.

Body testing is effective but slow because you have to know the right questions to ask or go through a binary yes/no question set to finally find the truth. In our certification training, we have a set of questions we teach to help our coaches find the exact resistance that's stopping someone from taking the correct action.

The second way I interact with the Superconscious is by getting clear messages. They are usually metaphors, symbols, sounds, images, stories, and sometimes a word. The Superconscious often sends the Unconscious information in the form of a symbol, metaphor, or picture. The message is always positive and never negative or literal.

I believe communication is done this way because the Superconscious has been communicating with the Unconscious since before language was introduced. It works with pre-verbal communication.

To ensure I get correct information from the Superconscious, I create a specific container for the information I'm after, and then I trust what I get. Once I have a symbol or message from the Superconscious, I must make up (or form) what it signifies. Invention is the most creative act there is.

We look up to people who have produced great artwork, businesses, marriages, health, books, and more. However, we have resistance to being *allowed* to "make it up." As a child, we were likely told off for "making it up." If you want to have a great working relationship with the Superconscious, you must MAKE IT UP and use your intuition. I will explain what this looks like later in the chapter.

Once you have the connection, you can simply ask or command the Superconscious to change the instructions or give you insight into the truth.

Let's give it a go.

## CREATING A BODY CONNECTION

Our first goal is to notice how our Superconscious wants to give us a "yes" or "no" command. If you remember our previous exercise, you were able to get a feeling from your body when something was a mistake and when something was correct. You will receive a "yes" or "no" from the Superconscious in a similar way.

First, let's create a "yes" feeling in our bodies.

Remember a time when you made a correct choice/decision. Close your eyes and imagine it. Notice what you feel, and experience it in your body. Become fluent with this feeling. When you are really feeling it, decide that this feeling will represent a "yes."

Now do the same for a "no."

Remember a time when you made an incorrect choice/ decision. Close your eyes and imagine it. Notice what you feel, and experience it in your body. Become fluent with this feeling. When you are really feeling it, decide that this feeling will represent a "no."

Please do not skip ahead in this process, as you will get the best results by going through these fully.

Next, close your eyes and connect to your heart. Let go of needing to know. Let go of the moment and just count your breaths as you take ten big slow breaths, focusing on your heart and feeling grateful for the moment. When you are done, open your eyes.

Now ask to connect to your Superconscious. Ask, "Superconscious, are you there?" Notice what you feel. Allow whatever is true to be there.

Now, let's create a container or structure for the information we wish to receive.

Give the command, "Superconscious, I want you to show me a 'yes' or a 'no.'"

Think of a decision you need to make.

Close your eyes and ask, "Superconscious, is this the right decision?"

Notice how you feel. Was it a "yes" or a "no"? What did you get? This process takes some practice, but once you are able to get a clear "yes" or "no" from your Superconscious, life becomes a whole lot easier.

## RECEIVING GUIDANCE

Now that you can connect to your Superconscious, you can receive information from the field, which is really fun. The key is allowing yourself to make it up and learning to trust what you get. It's an advanced process, and you don't need to learn how to do it to work with the Superconscious field. Having the ability to receive a "yes" and a "no" is more than enough.

That said, learning to receive guidance is the highest form of communicating with the Superconscious. Remember, what you receive is never negative or literal.

For example, I was once working with a client, and the guidance I saw was him killing a young boy. This was obviously not literal. It meant it was time for him to kill the inner boy and step into owning his life like a man. The guidance you receive is never literal; it is for you, and you must find your meaning.

## THE WISDOM PROCESS

There is a process for doing this, and we call it the "Wisdom Process." It starts off by deciding the end result/decision you want information on and then letting the Superconscious guide you to what is there. When you learn to get information from the field, life will never be the same again.

First, you access the Superconscious by going into innocence and your heart, and then you ask open-ended questions. By getting a symbol or metaphor or vision, you know you are working with the Superconscious.

Whatever you get, you must start writing down what it suggests. As you write the meaning, you may end up in a completely different place than you presumed. If you happen to get a vision of exactly what you think you are supposed to do, write that down. It may or may not change, but write it down, so you have it.

Let's go through the process step by step. The first thing to do is define what choice you want information on. Say, "I choose the end result of _____ " (start with one of the core four).

Next, connect to the Superconscious by dropping into your heart. Once you are connected to the Superconscious, you may want to muscle test or ask the question to ensure you feel connected.

Once connected, you will use open-ended questions to get a symbol, vision, or metaphor. Use open-ended questions like, "What are all the possible ways I could achieve this?" By doing this, you allow your Superconscious to go on a search of the field and come back with information for you. Once you have information, the next step is to decipher what it means.

The only way to decipher what it means is to interpret it through your imagination and make it up. Remember, you must allow yourself to make up what you are getting and what is coming through. Allow possibilities to be there, and allow yourself to flow.

To summarize, here are the steps of the Wisdom Process to receive guidance from your Superconscious:

1. Choose an end result you would like to create.
2. Connect to your heart and allow yourself to be present.
3. Close your eyes and visualize/accept the end result of this creation as true now.
4. Notice the current reality or current creation compared to that end result.
5. Ask for the Superconscious to give you a symbol, metaphor, or guidance on what needs to be done next.
6. Write down what you receive and what it means to you.

Now it's your turn. Grab a pen and paper and give this a go.

How was that?

Did you get something? It doesn't have to be much. We've only just begun!

Now, let's have fun working with our Superconscious to change instructions in our field and transform our reality.

## THE RECODE

You can use the Superconscious to treat/change any resistance you have to an end result you would like to manifest. We do this by using the Recode process.

When we are using the creative structure, we trigger resistance into the active experience through structural tension. Your active experience is everything you are consciously and Unconsciously experiencing right now. It is made up of thoughts, feelings, memories, desires, people, situations, and more.

When you decide to go for the desired reality and step into the emotion of having it, you will find that you're not 100 percent feeling good about taking the obliged action. This feeling is called resistance.

Resistance is not a bad thing. It's just a previous creation designed to keep you from ending up in painful situations.

It was put there by you to prevent you from ending up in a situation you previously thought was dangerous or unsafe. This is because the number one job of the Unconscious is to ensure you and your body survive.

This is not a bad thing, but this safety mechanism starts to hinder your life because the Unconscious decides that anything new is not safe. It decides it's not safe because it's unproven. From the Unconscious perspective, if you or your family have not lived through an experience, it's not as safe as the ones you have. So, the Unconscious sends "warning signs" in the form of uncomfortable feelings whenever you are about to do something new.

Of course, just because something is new doesn't make it unsafe. In fact, the new condition may actually be safer. In spite of logic, the Unconscious wants to keep everything the same. Therefore, whenever you create something new, there is a battle.

This battle is between your Self-Conscious that wants to create new realities and your Unconscious that wants to keep everything the same. Resistance is the mechanism the Unconscious uses to win the fight and keep everything the same.

**All resistance is a set of beliefs, thoughts, identities,**

**emotions, or other aspects of you that made a decision that was useful in the past.**

You may experience amnesia during this process of trying to find what is in the way. If you are unsure of where the resistance comes from, that is okay. If you just can't seem to follow through on a certain thing or create a certain outcome, but you don't know why, all you need to know is there is resistance. Your Superconscious can work the rest out. There is no need to try and dig up a lifetime of reasons why you can't achieve something. It's enough just to know there is a block.

When it comes to health, some people just can't seem to get the results they want. In relationships, people get triggered into saying things they don't mean. As you face resistance, you might feel like you have more than one personality: one that wants to do a certain action—forgive, go to the gym, meditate or make that phone call—and the other one wants to get angry, procrastinate, doubt, blame, or get anxious.

We have many sub-personalities, and most of them work together in harmony. You do not have the same personality while with your children, while at work, or even when you are out with your friends.

You are a different character with different values, speech

patterns, and outcomes. The problem arises when one of the sub-personalities is against the action another wants to take. For example, you have a sub-personality that is an achiever and another created to avoid all rejection.

These two will fight, and usually, the one that has experienced the most pain will win. You may have no recollection of this sub-personality. It may just be a feeling or a set of information passed down from generations. Either way, the resistance is there, and you would prefer it not to be.

Many times, a memory is the originator of the resistance. The memory is likely not part of the main personality. It could have been created in this lifetime or passed down through the family DNA. You have many dormant memories. You have no conscious awareness of them, but something in your life can trigger them into your active experience.

A dormant memory is one that is not in the active experience, and it can be triggered into the active experience easily. For example, do you remember where you were on September 11, 2001? Or can you remember the last time you rode a bicycle? Do you remember when you graduated from high school or university? Or the death or birth of someone you love? I am sure you answered "yes" to one or all of the above. You were obviously not thinking about them before I asked. Those memories were dormant, which proves you have many dormant memories outside your active experience.

You also have many patterns that run automatically. Speech, writing, and walking are complex patterns that involve many muscles, neurons, and systems.

However, your Unconscious runs the pattern the same way it runs a thought process.

Have you ever wondered if your thoughts were actually your own? Behind the Self-Conscious veil, there are literally billions of cell divisions, thoughts, feelings, and other automatic processes happening every second that you are not aware of. They have been learned in this lifetime, modeled from parents and passed down. Again, we do not need to know where they came from. We simply must notice they exist so we can Recode the information.

The Recode works by explaining to the Superconscious that this current pattern is not the pattern we desire to continue. Most think resistance is an enemy, but the truth is, all resistance, all patterns, and all information were for you.

It was very useful at one time.

For instance, a person abused by a stranger as a child creates a useful belief not to trust strangers. However, that belief now creates a negative effect for this person as an adult who wants to meet crowds of strangers to make sales and do business with them.

A baby elephant can be tied to a little rope and a small stake in the ground, and it will not be able to run away. This same elephant as an adult can be tied in the same way and not pull at all. They have learned helplessness, much the same way we do as humans.

However, we can Recode the information and, therefore, make new decisions. This is done by separating the emotion and content of a memory because emotion is the instruction to the Unconscious and causes the resistance.

Our Unconscious must learn what the truth is, let go of the pain, and grow more competent. But because the Unconscious takes everything personally, it usually misses the real learning and holds on to the pain for a lifetime.

This avoidance leads to more pain in life. If we can Recode the emotion and allow true learning to be present, the correct actions can be taken.

For example, you may have been rejected many times in your life. The rejections that stick with you are the ones with the most pain associated with them. The pain was created as a warning for the Unconscious to avoid that situation in the future. You may need to learn to do your best regardless of what others think. You may need to learn that people will reject you, and that's okay. Rejection doesn't change your worth. That's the real learning.

When we do the Superconscious work, we connect with the resistance and ask for it to be "treated," allowing true learning to take place.

The Recode works by changing all the instructions that cause resistance. This allows a different action to be taken. A good way to explain this is by thinking about an end result you have not been able to manifest.

Imagine the end result being at the end of a road. Because of past actions, the road is in disrepair and cannot be driven on. You notice potholes, and they stop you from being able to move forward. What needs to happen? You need to fix the road. Luckily, because you created all the resistance (potholes), you can easily fix or change them. As soon as you do, you can easily move to what you desire. Or, put in a different way, your Superconscious will remember how these potholes came into existence, and in the perfect way and perfect order will fill them in and smooth them over, allowing you to easily move to your end result.

How much you acknowledge and change resistance is up to you. This process is about creating results you desire, not being perfect. However, if that old pattern is in the way of what you desire, I suggest getting new information. The old information was valid, but it's not useful anymore. You can be amazing with a sword, but it's useless in a gunfight. The yellow pages might have helped you find a dentist in the past, but now you can just go online and search for one. It doesn't matter how useful the original information was; the question is, will it help you in the future? I think of resistance like a vampire, sucking the life out of what we want to create. As soon as we shine some light on it, it evaporates into nothingness.

With the Superconscious Recode, you can Recode any resistance in your identity and have what you desire. You can be it so you can see it. You don't need to change your whole self, fix the past, or try to be perfect. You simply need to focus on what you desire and notice what is in the way. Once you determine what is in the way, you can connect to your Superconscious and change the coding.

I like to say this process is like having a "river of desire." At the end of the river is the land of plenty with everything you would love to see manifest, and you are in the current reality of the current in the river.

As you move towards what you desire, some boulders pop up and stop the flow of the river, making it impossible to flow to what you desire.

These boulders can easily be removed by remembering when they were useful and choosing to smooth them over or roll them away so a new flow can happen. This process is very easy and gentle, and you will experience profound shifts.

Occasionally, the resistance is too much to move in one session. Too much of the identity is caught up in it. It's like there's a huge boulder the size of a car in the way of the end result. Instead of trying to remove it all in one go, we simply ask the Superconscious to Recode a small part over multiple sessions until there is no resistance left.

In this case, you let your Superconscious know to chisel a piece off and remove a little part at a time. After a few sessions, the whole boulder is moved. There is no need to rush.

You know a Recode has worked when what was stopping you from moving towards your end result is no longer a problem. We are not sitting still, asking what is wrong with us and trying to fix it. Instead, we are in momentum, moving towards a result we would love, and we are aligning with that.

In this process, you get to be a creator, you get to have it all, and be in love with creating more things you love. This is the reason why we are on this planet, to experience our creative energy and witness ourselves creating! You are always creating, and you always have been; now you are just taking control of that function.

## TRIAL SUPERCONSCIOUS RECODE

This exercise will be a test/trial/practice Recode session, which is how we use the Superconscious to remove resistance and unwanted feelings towards the desired end result.

I invite you to follow this exercise that will introduce you to the world of the Superconscious and what is possible. Later, we will move on and do the process with all your true choices, but first, it's important to learn to Recode your resistance and connect with your Superconscious.

The end result of our test/trial/practice session is for you to witness a change. It's best to work on something you have a "charge" on but isn't central to your identity.

A charge is a heightened emotion above what is normally necessary. Working on the anxiety of public speaking or fear of an insect or animal makes for a great test session because the identity doesn't have to give much up to experience the Recode. There is not much at stake, and most aspects agree it's a good thing to Recode the instructions.

So, pick something you have a charge on that doesn't have huge identity resistance. You can use the examples above or think of a negative emotion that is sometimes triggered for you. The trigger might happen in a close relationship (you get so annoyed when ___ does ____), or it might occur with certain circumstances (you see ___ on the news, and you feel ___).

The reason we are choosing something with a charge is so you can experience the shift. I would like for you to choose something with a charge of about a six or seven out of ten, with ten being the highest negative emotion you could feel.

Once you have decided on your focus, please write it down. "The test session I will be focused on _____.

The resistance I feel is a ____ out of ten.

Once you have chosen your test, set a clear end result of how you would like to feel instead. For example, "When I see a spider, I choose to feel calm and centered" or "When I speak on stage, I chose to feel natural and confident."

Go ahead and write that down.

"I choose to feel _____ when _____."

Now we're going to "collapse the wave of possibilities" and choose this end result. Do this by closing your eyes, choosing this reality, and experiencing it in the invisible. So, close your eyes, use your imagination to step into the reality you desire, choose to have it, accept it as true, and experience it.

What is it like? How does it feel? How great would it be to have this reality? Witness yourself at that moment the exact way you desire, staying in the end result for at least twenty seconds.

If you haven't already, please close your eyes and do it now.

Did you do it?

Did it feel good?

Yes?

Okay, so now we want to figure out what is stopping you from feeling that way all the time. You will do this by dropping into the "current reality" into the current of the river of desire—where you are now.

Imagine the end result is a shooting star, and you are experiencing the "tail" of it, where it started. It's time to experience the now and create the perfect structure.

Ask yourself:

Compared to the reality I desire, what is it like now?

Where am I now?

What have I created compared to what I desire?

What thoughts and feelings do I have?

How am I defining myself? Others? And the world?

What conflicts do I have?

How do I finish the sentence "It would be really nice to have that result, but I can't because _____"?

Write down your answers.

Now that you have allowed the resistance to come into the active experience, you need to own that you are the Superconscious creator, and you created all of this.

All resistance was useful at some time. Note that I said it was "useful." Not right, not wrong. It was just useful to you or someone who came before you. We do not need to know why it is there, just that it is.

It's time to change the instructions, so the resistance is no longer there. Let's connect to the Superconscious.

To connect, I want you to drop into the field of your heart

by closing your eyes and taking a few big breaths. Picture a small baby or child having fun playing with a small furry kitten. Watch the joy in their face and experience how it is for them in that moment. Connect to their playful joy in the moment, and witness a part of yourself in them as you remember what it was like to be a child (or make it up).

Remember what you love, and remember you have an imagination. With each breath, allow yourself to connect with your heart. Connect with these two beautiful young energies and feel joy for no reason at all as you drop deeper into your heart. Allow yourself to sit there for a moment or two.

Close your eyes and do it now.

Now, ask to connect to your Superconscious and get a sensation in the body to signal a "yes."

Say, "Superconscious, are you there? Can you show me a yes?" Notice what changes as you ask it. This is your yes.

Close your eyes and do it now.

Command your Superconscious to treat all the resistance to the end result you are creating. Ask it to treat the original event and all emotions, thoughts, and beliefs that are stopping the natural flow.

"Superconscious, please treat all resistance, including the original event, emotions, thoughts, feelings, and beliefs."

Close your eyes and say the above sentence in your mind.

Now, wait a few moments and notice what is different (you will likely feel or sense a calm energy flow through you).

When you feel it is right, ask your Superconscious if there is any resistance left over that needs to be treated today.

"Superconscious if there is any resistance left that needs to be treated today, please treat it."

Wait a few moments, then step back into your end result. Experience the end result again as you would like it. Close your eyes and imagining yourself experiencing it in the perfect emotion. Notice what is different. Notice how you feel.

Ask yourself, "What is different? What has changed?"

Open your eyes and think about your end result and how you would like to be in that state in the future. What level of resistance do you have to being that way the next time you have the same experience? How will you feel if you are asked to speak in public? Or the next time a spider crawls in front of you? Or the next time that old, triggered emotion comes up?

Do you feel the same or different? Has the resistance dropped?

What number is it out of ten?

You likely had at least a small drop in your resistance, and you've had your first experience of using your Superconscious to Recode the resistance.

It's very cool, isn't it? There is more still, but first, I want to say, great job! Welcome to the world of the Superconscious. If you have completed this chapter, you have learned how to connect to your Superconscious, receive guidance, and do the Recode. This forms a large part of our full system. You are well on your way to living Superconsciously.

Remember, this is your very first go at it, and you will get a lot better, so even if you only feel a slight or small change, it's a start!

Now that you have done a practice session, if you would like to try a Recode on one of the core four choices, you can. Or, jump into the next chapter, where we will dive in even further.

To work on one of the core four choices, simply redo this process with the choice as the theme of the end result instead of the charged emotion.

For clarity, we use the charged emotion in the practice session to get used to the idea. We never go looking for resistance or problems. That's just crazy!

Instead, as we focus on our choice, we notice what is stopping us. Then, we use this process to Recode that resistance. The key is to ensure you are focused on what you are creating.

We will now only focus on creating. There is a big difference between building yourself to become a confident public speaker versus healing social anxiety. The latter is focused on the need to fix and gives no clear instructions on what you are creating.

By creating the end result we love, the old problem will not exist anymore. However, by trying to just fix the old "problem reality," we only give it power, which will never work long term.

By connecting to the Superconscious, you can change anything that doesn't serve what you wish to create. You can also use it to gain insight into living your truth and gaining insight from the unified field. There is so much information available in the field. You can learn to use it to guide you towards what is right for you.

In the next chapter, we will uncover what you really love.

You will learn to open the wizard's gate and own the magnetic moment.

## CHAPTER 6 REVIEW

To connect to the Superconscious, you must drop down into your heart, access innocence, and stop needing to know everything. To really see the truth, you must learn to stop needing to know how it is and go into a childlike place of presence, awe, openness, and innocence.

Our process of communicating with the Superconscious looks like this:

1. Go into innocence/drop into your heart,
2. Connect with the Superconscious through direct communication,
3. Get information through a message/symbol.

By connecting to the Superconscious, you can change anything that is not serving what you wish to create. You can also use it to gain insight into living your truth and gaining insight from the unified field. There is so much information available, and you can learn to use it to guide you towards what is right for you.

When you live the core four choices, you have mastered the magnetic moment, and you can then decide what you really love.

By using the Superconscious to decipher what you love, you are much more effective at creating because you no longer create two waves of information in the field. You have all your focus on just the one thing you desire to create, instead of having half of your focus on what you want and the other half elsewhere.

Resistance is not a bad thing. It is just a previous creation designed to keep you from ending up in painful situations. It has acted as a guiding system to keep you safe. However, it is now the opposing force of the action you desire to take. It can show up as a feeling, a thought, or simply as an Unconscious block.

**All resistance is a set of beliefs, thoughts, identities, emotions, or other aspects of you that made a decision that was useful in the past.**

# CHAPTER 7

---•◦•---

# TRUE CHOICES

When you are really living the core four choices, you may find you no longer desire many of your old goals. This is because many of them were negative visions designed by your Unconscious as a way to complete you. They were designed by your limited perspective to solve a problem you believed to be true about you (usually one of the six core negative beliefs). A negative vision is the opposite of a true choice, and we will discuss the seven focus points that create a negative vision in this chapter.

In short, most people do not have true choices because they have spent a lifetime ignoring or editing their true desires.

Just because you are living the core four choices does not make you a conscious creator. It makes you satisfied and happy. However, humans are not designed just to be happy.

We are designed to go on an adventure of creating and experiencing conditions and circumstances that matter—ones that light us up on the inside and that we love.

Living the four choices is just a milestone on your adventure of a lifetime to create a life you love.

After a few years of working with my Superconscious, I was happy, content, and satisfied with life. I was able to arrive at any circumstances and feel the same; I had mastered the moment. However, I wasn't creating. I was still living out negative visions and intentions I thought were true choices, but in reality, they were not.

After Deas died, I got myself into multiple business partnerships that did not work out. I was trying to fill the void Deas left in the company and in my life. I was living from a limited belief that I couldn't build the business on my own. Each partnership I entered became increasingly worse, until I was broke in Austin, Texas, after yet another terrible partnership break-up.

I thought I was doing everything right. I treated all the negative emotions and allowed myself to feel good, spending a few months in Texas on a mini-vacation. I was living in the moment; I was happy and loving life. But I wasn't creating.

With our lease coming to an end, my wife and I needed to

make a decision about what would happen next in our life. We looked at many places to live in many different states. We knew we did not want to stay in Austin because of the pain of running into this ex-business partner. New Zealand? Australia? We could go anywhere.

We decided the best move was to head to my wife's home country of England. We rationalized that it would allow us some quality time with her family when the truth was, it was just a safe and easy option. We moved to the country-side of England, living with my wife's brother, walking our dogs each day. We had a small online business that made enough for us to live on. We felt happy and content. Yet something was missing.

One day, as I was out walking and feeling great, I had this sense of sadness come over me. I can't explain it, but it was like I was longing for or missing something, but at the same time, I was just so content. I couldn't understand it. There was no problem to solve, yet there was something else I needed.

I didn't know it at the time, but the goal isn't just to be happy. This is because we desire more than that. Humans are obsessed with one thing, and you can see it in all sports, movies, plays, dramas, and in our life journey: we are after an adventure. We desire to go out into the world on a quest to get somewhere, overcome the odds, and create a result we love.

Heading home and explaining it to Harriet, we decided to sit and create new choices for our life.

We sat down and started with our life choices, using a predictable process that we will cover in this chapter.

After connecting into our Superconscious and choosing the core four, we started on our other choices, asking for a symbol/vision for the end result of "creating a business that changes the world." I asked Harriet what she got, and she said, "S." I said, "Me too!"

Then I asked her, "What did that mean to you?" She turned her page to me, and it read: *speaking business*. At this point, I was laughing my head off. I showed her that I had written *seminar business*.

We both got the symbol of an "S," and we both interpreted it the same way. The problem was, I didn't want to start a speaking business. I had tried that before and spent too much time away from my family. I had failed at that and had made up my mind to build a "real business." I was living in the English countryside and hadn't planned on building anything other than an online marketing company, so we ignored it.

The next end result we tuned into was the end result of our perfect home. I got the image of a big house by the beach close to an airport, lots of sun, big open spaces, water views, solar panels, and space for my dogs to run around. Harriet got something very similar. Writing it down, we both felt a sense of impossibility, as there was nothing like that in England. Beaches and sun? *Not possible*, we thought.

As we continued the process, we kept receiving messages that just weren't possible. We chose to ignore them, and instead of starting the "S" business and living by the beach, we moved to London.

We tried to justify the move as "being close to nature," as we had moved to Hampstead Heath outside of London, which is a beautiful part of the world. However, as we trudged through the icy winter weather, we knew it was not our end result.

This was not the guidance we received. We were not following through. We were trying to have everything "make sense." We were living out of reaction and limitation.

About six weeks after the move, we received a letter from the Immigration Department stating I had been refused my Visa. We had not met the income criteria due to having a business that was only two years old (it was the same business we had been running for years, and we had just restarted it, but it didn't matter in this case). I had thirty days to leave the country. I could only challenge the decision outside of England; however, an appeal could take six to twelve months.

Sitting in disbelief, we felt like our world had been pulled out from under us. We had only moved to England the year before, and we loved being close to Harriet's family. The thought of moving with two dogs and establishing ourselves in a new country again felt grueling.

Harriet is English, and I'm from New Zealand, so we knew Australia was the logical choice for the move. Previous residence in Australia for five years gained Harriet her long-term Visa, and I had automatic access as a New Zealander.

So, we decided that was where we would go. From all perspectives, it looked like the move was going to be horrible. I had less than four weeks until I had to leave England. Even more heartbreaking was the fact that our dogs had to have a six-month quarantine without us. With the added pressure of running a business and the multiple failures I'd had before, I was stressed out of my mind as I formulated a plan. I felt like a total failure. A part of me wondered if Harriet would even bother joining me in Australia because, at this point, nothing was going right.

I boarded a plane for Australia within a week, intending to find a place to live and because we needed to make extra money to pay for the unexpected expense of moving.

I reached out to some of my old business contacts in Australia and organized a series of workshops/speaking events. I wasn't in Australia for even a week before we put on the first event, and it was a big success both financially and emotionally. In the middle of all this mess, I had something I knew how to do and could make great money fast.

I rented a small place, and for a month, I worked my butt off running events, making money, and getting us set up. Harriet packed up the house and found a farm for our dogs to stay in for six months of luxury quarantine. She also closed businesses, said goodbye to family, and did the million other things that needed to be done. After that month, she arrived to a brand-new business in a brand-new country.

Six months later, our dogs arrived, and we moved into our perfect house at Palm Beach with a huge backyard. It was a fifteen-minute ride to the airport, and we had our own private beach. We had events every weekend, and our income had doubled!

If we had listened to our truth and not to our fear, we would have taken the correct action earlier and saved a lot of pain.

When you follow the five steps, your wildest dreams will come true. Even if the goals or visions seem completely impossible, when you follow your heart and align your Superconscious, your true end results manifest like magic.

If you listen and follow through, you will have a much easier time than if you ignore what you get.

For us, if we had just listened in the first place to what our hearts and intuition were telling us, we would have ended up in Australia with far less trouble and stress, and we wouldn't have wasted a huge amount of money.

From that moment on, I decided I would follow my truth, no matter what.

This was not the only time I had been in awe of the Superconscious. In November 2019 I was doing this process and got a clear vision of the US Map, followed by a YouTube symbol.

I started writing what it meant and decided I needed to create a YouTube ad with the US as a target market. This was an entirely crazy idea at that time. I had no clients in the USA, lived in Australia, and had never created a YouTube ad.

This time, I followed the instructions even though they seemed crazy again. I did some searching, got some instructions, and turned on the ad in late October.

The month before the YouTube ad, our company had generated $100,000 in sales, and I felt quite good about that.

But what happened next was amazing. The YouTube ad went viral, and new sales increased by over $300,000 in one month!

It made no sense at all!

Even if the instructions don't make sense, you'll see them come true!

When you get a clear message, it's always a positive instruction: "do this." It is never "don't do ___." It usually comes in the form of a symbol you need to decipher for meaning, and sometimes it comes as a clear image of the end result. Whatever you get, you need to ignore your doubts and perceived limitations.

When you follow through on the instructions, you will receive end results that impact you and others at the same time.

One day, after a huge month of running events and promotions, I sat exhausted, flicking through Facebook messages. I had received multiple messages from one of my students asking me to work with him. He wanted to work one-on-one with me, which was not something I typically offered.

He was persistent, so I connected into my Superconscious and asked, "What should I say to him?" The answer I got was "yes," so I reluctantly took him on as a client.

A month later, I was on an all-expenses-paid business class flight to LA to meet this client, who, unbeknownst to me at that time, was a member of one of the top 2,000 richest families in the world.

His mother was in total gratitude after I worked with her son, and I was able to ask her some meaningful questions only a self-made billionaire could answer. The answers I received changed my whole perspective on what is possible, who we are, and how the world works. I would not have had access to these answers without following my Superconscious intuition.

By learning to listen to the Superconscious, your results will happen faster. It will seem like magic.

## LET GO OF TRYING TO WORK IT ALL OUT SO YOU CAN LEARN THE TRUTH

Getting information from the Superconscious field is always going to be faster than trying to use your Self-Conscious. This is because your Self-Conscious only uses your lifetime experience to make decisions, whereas the Superconscious is connected to infinite intelligence. It's obvious which aspect will make the better decision.

Listening to the instructions and following through is the hard part because your thoughts and feelings will lie to you. Your Self-Conscious and Unconscious do not understand the Superconscious.

Your Self-Conscious perspective thinks it can work everything out. It thinks it knows everything, and it doesn't believe in miracles. Our collective Self-Conscious perspectives have been trying to understand the miracle of human existence, and we've been struggling for centuries.

Imagine if, in order for anything to be true or valid, we had to work it all out. It's funny to think about that, but this part of us really believes, "If I don't understand it, it can't be possible." To our Self-Conscious, everything must make sense.

Your Self-Conscious wants clear, linear steps. It likes to know how things are, and it doesn't want to make errors. So, the idea of following through on guidance from the Superconscious can seem ludicrous.

The problem is, the Self-Conscious can't understand the infinite potentials of the universe.

In order to be Self-Conscious, our consciousness must observe itself as separate from the world around it. To do this, it must forget that it is more than this. This process of forgetting is needed to have our human experience, yet it causes many challenges. One of these challenges is the reliance on thoughts and feelings.

Thoughts and feelings are based on memories picked up in this lifetime and are totally limited because they are only based on this one lifetime. The Superconscious does not have thoughts or feelings. It is a field of all information, so to become Superconscious, you must let go of your thoughts and feelings.

Strangely, our Self-Conscious believes it knows better than the Superconscious. It thinks that if it doesn't understand it, then it must not be valid or accurate!

All your new knowledge lies outside of what you already know. By needing to know everything, you slow down your ability to learn what you don't know and to receive the truth. If you want the truth, you must allow yourself not to know. Allow yourself to receive what is there without judging or trying to work it out.

It sounds funny, but the Self-Conscious Ego thinks it can use Newtonian reasoning and break everything down into pieces. By understanding a small piece of something, then it can understand the whole. The absurdity of this is obvious. Imagine trying to understand a human being by examining a strand of hair!

What's the result of the Self-Conscious? When you get genius ideas, it will lie to you and try to say the idea is stupid or won't work. It will try to create a narrative or look for proof. It will always try to plan and work everything out. It believes it knows what is possible.

The Self-Conscious is very good at knocking you out of the Superconscious field, and you must not give it that power!

Your Unconscious, on the other hand, is the domain of feelings. It keeps a record of the past and helps you make decisions in the present.

Remember those shortcuts that tell us whether something is right or wrong for us? What has been determined to be right or wrong is simply based on how we survived. The Unconscious only has one desire—to keep the body alive; therefore, it looks to repeat past conditions.

Because of the Unconscious, you cannot make decisions without feeling the right way. For example, when you see an attractive person on the other side of the bar and want to talk to them, you will likely feel a shot of fear.

This fear makes no sense, as the other person is probably nice and would engage in a conversation. However, your fear of being rejected is stronger than the logic, and you decide it's safer to just order another drink and stay with the people you know.

Your emotions are the decision-makers in your body and have no basis in reality.

What is great about the Unconscious is that it can easily be reprogrammed. You can use the emotion of the end result to teach the Unconscious that the future you desire is safe. This is vital to understand and to create a flowing structure rather than an oscillating one.

In reprogramming the Unconscious, we ensure there is no emotional difference between the now and the desire.

When there is no emotional difference, then the correct action can occur. If you feel good standing at the bar with your friends and feel good walking up to the attractive person, you have no resistance. So, if you want to, you just take action.

As you decide to follow through on the things that really matter to you, old patterns of information and former decisions will pop into your active experience, causing resistance. You must learn to stay focused on the end results and "leave the baby crying."

Many of us feel the need to race and fix any resistance we feel as we are creating, but unlike a real baby, your internal baby does not need your attention. You need to follow through anyway.

We live in a world where any sense of discomfort is avoided. As you are pushing your limits and stepping into new possibilities, your Unconscious will cry out, "You can't do this; it's too much. You don't even really want it. What will people think of you? You're not ready." You must leave it crying.

The Unconscious is designed to keep things the same. So, if the Unconscious is happy all the time, you are not on the edge of creation, which is where you want to be, at least some of the time. Everything you truly want is on the other side of what your identity believes it is and what it believes is safe. As you go for it, there comes a point where your identity must give up its ways of being, but it will fight to keep its old patterns.

It will literally kick and scream to keep its limitations—like a baby. Again, you must leave it crying. You must step into the end result, notice the crying, notice the resistance, Recode it, and follow through. You don't try to work it out; you simply LET IT GO. You Recode that shit and move on!

By doing this, you put a light on the vampire—your limiting belief. The belief cannot survive if you are living in a state contrary to it.

For example, you might begin to feel the pull of "not being enough." The antidote is to sit in "enoughness," and as soon as you do, the part of you that was scared of it realizes you can exist in this reality. The belief cannot hold, and just like the vampire, it is obliterated.

You must leave your inner child crying for attention and go for what you want.

## DISCOVERING WHAT YOU WOULD REALLY LOVE TO CREATE

What do you really love?

Most of us have not answered this question in a long time and are going for things we think we should have, think we should be, or what is expected.

If you have ever been to a seminar where the lecturer makes you write all sorts of materialistic dreams, and you thought, "I don't really want all of this," you were right!

You don't. You don't really want the images you cut out from a glossy magazine and put on a vision board.

There is nothing wrong with having them, but first, you must live your true choices in a creative structure, completely happy with the now. Ultimately, that is what you really want. If you are not living a life you love now, you will always be in the wrong structure! When you finally get into the right structure, and there is no resistance to any end result, you can then create material things with ease (they are actually the easiest to manifest).

It's likely you have never asked yourself:

- What do I really love?
- What do I really want from life?
- What is my true dream?

Let's do a little exercise to help you step into the difference between your identity/Self-Conscious and your Superconscious genius so you can find true choices that you love.

1. First, think of one thing you would really love to create more than anything in the world (just pick one).
2. Now, close your eyes and step into your Superconscious field. Witness what you really love as true, from the perspective of your heart. Notice what it's like to just have it for no reason at all other than loving it. Feel what it's like from this perspective.
3. Open your eyes for a moment, and then close them again. This time, witness the same end result from the perspective of your Self-Conscious/identity. What do you believe having this end result will change for you? What do you need to do to get it? What would happen to you if you lost it?
4. What is the difference between the two? Can you notice the different feelings between your truth and your vision to compensate for feeling "not enough"?

In doing this exercise, when you experience a choice from your heart, it likely feels easy. Everything flows, and there is no resistance to having it. When you experience it from your identity, you may feel worried about losing it and excited only if you get it. It may feel like having it changes you. If you really went for it and "failed," that would mean something to your identity, so you may avoid it and just go for other things where this risk is not present.

Through doing this exercise, we can see why our goals don't manifest. We are creating them from a limited perspective of the identity, which tries to problem-solve and fix. This is not the creative reality.

Here's what happens when you're not creating your true choices: If you really went for something and "failed," that would imply something to your identity. So, you avoid it and just go for things where this risk is not present.

Put differently, if you really went for your highest expression and didn't get it, your unwanted belief about yourself of not belonging, being insignificant, not capable, not worthy, not good enough, or not perfect would show up as being correct. So, you edit your true end results and, instead, go for things to solve the ways you feel incomplete.

**A true end result is something you desire to create for no reason other than you would love to see it created.**

## SEVEN FOCUS POINTS THAT KEEP YOU AWAY FROM A TRUE CHOICE AND STUCK IN A NEGATIVE VISION

In helping thousands create true end results/choices, I know there are predictable ways that we actually create negative visions instead of true end results that we love. I will explain these in-depth, so you know what to look out for. These seven focus points are the motivators behind the goals, and they knock you out of a true choice. They are:

### I. RESOLVE A NEGATIVE BELIEF
YOUR GOAL IS ABOUT COMPLETING A WAY YOU FEEL INCOMPLETE.

I am not worthy, so I will make all my goals about others, the world, and society. Once I am good enough, I will be worthy and can have what I want.

I am not good enough, so I will set goals to achieve and prove to others I am good enough.

I am insignificant, so all my goals will be about creating significance. Or, I won't have any goals because if I went for them and didn't achieve them, I would prove I'm insignificant.

I don't belong, so I will set goals to fit in, be attractive enough to be loved, or create something to belong to. I will avoid rejection at all costs and reject others first, so I'm never the one rejected.

I don't have the capability, so all goals will be about creating enough resources to finally be able to do what I desire. My life will be about having enough knowledge, money, relationships, time, or other resources to finally live my life. I am willing to lose my truth in the search for these resources.

I am not perfect, and I need to be perfect. I need to control myself and how the world and others see me. I must be perfect because only perfect people succeed. All my goals will be about how I need to be, act, feel, and think.

## 2. REACTION

YOUR GOAL IS ACTUALLY A DESIRE TO GET AWAY FROM AN UNWANTED CIRCUMSTANCE OR CONDITION. "I AM GOING TO DO _____ BECAUSE OF _____."

Here's an example: I got fired, so I will start a business. Or, I feel overweight, so I am going to the gym.

The problem with this is all the motivation is stored in a negative situation, and a small amount of success will kill the momentum.

To expand on the above examples, as soon as you no longer feel overweight, the motivation to go to the gym is gone. Or, you realize you don't really want all the stress of a business and go back to a regular office job. In either case, you didn't really want the end result, so you weren't ready to do what it takes to make it happen.

You can also have future reactions. This is when we look at all the things we don't want and then make a decision based on that. "I don't want to _____, so that means I will go for _____."

Some people say it this way: "I don't know what I want, but I know what I don't want."

This creates a complete focus on what is unwanted, which just gives away power.

Just because you don't want a crappy boss doesn't mean you want to own a business.

Just because you don't want to be unhealthy doesn't mean you love going to the gym every day.

Reacting to the negative gives all the power away to the negative, instead of having power in the creation.

### 3. LIMITATION
YOUR GOAL IS ACTUALLY FOCUSED ON WHAT YOU THINK IS POSSIBLE FOR YOU, NOT ON WHAT YOU WOULD REALLY LOVE. YOU HAVE EDITED DOWN YOUR DREAM.

This sounds like: "I really want _____ but I am going to aim for _____ because I believe that is actually possible.

This person usually has reduced their goals to almost nothing. They want to avoid disappointment at all costs, so they set the bar low. They do nothing for what they really love.

E.g., I would love to be superabundant and rich; however, I am only after $100,000 income, and I would be happy with that.

This removes all the emotion out of the end result and reduces inspiration massively. In fact, you're telling your Superconscious you don't really believe in yourself or that it's bad to have what you really want. Limited goals are not true goals. They are based on what we think is possible. There is no emotion in that.

A lot of teachers say, "be specific," and this is good advice. The more precise you are, the better. However, this only holds if you apply it to what you really want/love. In our example above, a better goal would be "I choose to have more money than I can spend." Can you feel the emotional difference in this?

Behind limitation sits beliefs like, "I don't have what it takes to create what I desire, or to be the fullest expression of myself and love my life. Instead, I'll just go for a limited or small part of what I really want."

Go for your truth. Whatever substance it is, whatever is right, just go for it!!

## 4. OTHERS' OPINIONS

YOUR GOAL IS DESIGNED TO ENSURE OTHERS ARE HAPPY.

You only create goals based on what others think or what they will think about the result. Typically, there is a specific group or person whose opinion we care about most. This focus on what others think shows up as "Everyone thinks_____ is a good idea, so I will do it." Or "If I achieve _____ then others will think_____."

Here's an example: All my family said investing in property is a good idea, so I will do that to make them proud.

The challenge with this view is the end result is not yours, so you don't really own it. You set it up to be others' liability if it doesn't work out, and you are not trusting your own ability to know what is right for you. It's very confusing to the Superconscious if you are not going for what you want and only propose to make others happy.

## 5. CONTROL

HERE, YOUR GOALS MUST SHOW UP IN THE EXACT WAY YOU WANT THEM; YOU ARE NOT OPEN TO THE END RESULT.

Usually, the control is in the time frame, the circumstances, or the people. Sometimes a person who can't let go of control never gets what they desire because all their goals require other people to meet certain conditions.

E.g., I must have a loving relationship with _____, and they must treat me in a specific way, or I will not be happy.

Notice the lack of power in the above statement and the lack of free will. What if this particular person chooses not to behave in that way? What if that person lies or cheats? What if they die?

A better choice is: I choose a loving relationship that makes me feel great.

Can you feel the freedom and space in this? It could be the same person filling the desire of the relationship, but the creator defining this choice starts a very different energy with the slight change in the two statements.

There's a big difference between "I must have a happy marriage with [spouse name]" and "I choose a loving relationship that makes me feel great."

A person creating this way is not actually after the end result; they are after controlling everything because if they really just wanted the end result, then they would be happy however it turns up.

Here is another example of control when it comes to time: I will have _____ in exactly _____ months' time.

By imposing conditions, you try to control how you get your end results. Instead of allowing the true end result to manifest in the best way, this control creates stress and knocks you out of the emotion of the end result. It also knocks you out of the possibilities that exist and makes things very hard.

Does it really matter how the money shows up? Could it turn up faster than you want? Could you be open to creating the best upbringing for your children, instead of it having to be a certain way?

Many face this problem when building a business! They are not open to the many ways to have financial freedom; they just want it the way they want it.

They are not after the end result; they are after control.

## 6. INDIRECTNESS

YOUR GOALS ARE THE VEHICLES YOU HAVE CREATED TO GET YOU SOMEWHERE ELSE. YOU ARE TAKING THE LONG ROUTE.

Many try to plan their way to achieve everything. They like to think they know exactly what they must do to get somewhere, but they often get lost in what they think they must do, losing what they really want in the process.

The fallacy of the "find your why" movement has created the idea that we do something to get something else. The problem with this is we lose our true end result by going the roundabout way.

"I am creating _____ so that I can have _____."

For example, someone might say, "I created a business to create a good life for my kids."

In the example above, the person wants a good life for their kids, so they started a business. However, it's possible that while building the business, they miss having time with their children. They start working late nights and early mornings. They get caught up in the process and miss what they really wanted.

They missed the truth. If they just got into the end result of a great life for their children, maybe having a nine-to-five job would have been better. Who knows?

If this person had the end result as the focus, they would not have gone off-track in the process.

Many do this with education. They spend forever learning new techniques to finally be good at something, only to realize they could have started doing what they learned along the way and gotten to the end result faster.

Indirectness wastes time.

Later, we will cover the fastest way to get from where you are to what you want to create using your Superconscious. You will be blown away.

Go for what you want instead of taking a long way!

## 7. DEFAULT

THIS PERSON DOESN'T REALLY HAVE GOALS AND THINKS WHAT THEY HAVE IS "ENOUGH."

They say, "I have everything I desire now; I don't need anything else" or "I just take it as it comes; I don't need goals."

Sitting in the default position of having no goals won't get you the life you really want because the universe doesn't work that way. If you have no tension between here and what you love, you have created a void, and this void will be filled. If you are here to create more of what you love, you must have creative tension. Life is always moving. It's an action sport. If you are not the active, powerful creator of what you desire, you will be an element in others' ambitions.

Many think just because they have a great life, they have nothing left to create, and that is just not true. Life is about creating what you love, and just because you have a life you love now doesn't mean you can't create more. In fact, it's exactly *why* you get to create more.

As you can see from these seven focus points, most people's goals are really negative visions and are not true end results that they love. If you try to create anything under one of the above focuses, you will become very frustrated (you may have already experienced this). Instead, we create the core four orientations, step into a life we love first and then use the Superconscious to ask what we would love to create, for no other reason than we would love it.

Sometimes, when I coach people to create a life they love, a very interesting belief comes into their active experience: I am not allowed to love my life. They have an instruction coded up that has made loving life a bad thing. If that happens to you when we step into the exercises that follow, just know you are not alone!

The next step is to use the Superconscious differently and gain "insight" into your true choices. What would you really love?

The truth is, you can have everything you want, and you can be anything you desire. You are the creative energy. After all, you create it all!

Before moving ahead, consider the one or two focus points that keep you from your true choices. For me, it is indirectness. I tend to go for something to get me somewhere else. I spent years building a business big enough to feel worthy of being a mentor of Conscious Creation. If I just went for what I really wanted, I would have saved years.

## WHAT WOULD YOU LOVE TO CREATE?

There is only one way to be in a true choice, and that is to go for things you love—end results you choose to create for no other reason than you'd love to create them.

Start by claiming the biggest choices you can. This allows you to get in the energy of that choice; then, you break it down into small milestones you can focus on.

Usually, people have five to eight end results that are "true for them." These are things they really love, and no two are identical. However, there are some common themes:

- What family environment you wish to create
- What fulfills you
- What you are passionate about/things you love to do
- What art you love to create (art is anything you make for the joy of it)
- What you love to do for fun
- Your intimate relationship
- The home you would love to live in
- Your friendships
- Your perfect week/what you spend your time on
- Experiences you wish to have

- How you desire to serve/impact the world
- Your spiritual connection
- How much financial abundance you create
- What you do for a career/business

In all of these, the prime question is, "What would I really love to create?"

You are not asking how you will get there. There are no limits, no conditions—just true end results you love to create.

## BREAKING IT DOWN

A huge challenge people face when becoming Conscious Creators is they have never actually allowed themselves to create what they love. They base everything on what they thought was possible, to solve a problem, or go after what they were told was good.

Once you have decided on the true end results you would love to create, you can then break them down and focus on creating in a systematic and structured way.

We call this process the "Lenses Creation Process" because you are looking at one thing in varying degrees of focus. By changing the lens on a camera, you see in different ways.

For example, you choose the end result of financial abundance. This is the biggest lens in that structure. It is a true choice because there is no reason to have it other than it would be wonderful.

However, it is hard to act on such a big choice, so we break it down into a ninety-day objective.

We create a thirty-day target, a seven-day plan, and a daily ritual.

The reason we do this is to follow the natural rhythm of creation. A year is the total number of days the Earth orbits around the sun. Ninety days is approximately a season, and a month is an approximate lunar cycle.

The weeks fit into the month, and the days into the week. By using the natural rhythms, you tap into a big field structure.

Extra tip: start the year on your birthday to connect with your natural life rhythms.

Breaking your big vision down through lenses allows the structure to flow. If you complete your day, it bundles into your week and your month, and then eventually, the end result is manifested.

This is Superconscious creating.

So, let's get started on creating your end results. To do this, we will go into a possibility-imagination meditation with the core four orientation choices. To gather everything that is possible, we will ask for guidance from our Superconscious.

By doing it this way, you are coming from a place of creation, not problem-solving, and you gather true end results that you just love. Start with the first core choice, "I choose to love my life."

1.  Connect to your heart / Superconscious/ intuition and feel the moment
2.  Choose the end result of a life you love and feel it
3.  Ask, "What are all the possible ways I can have this?"
4.  Notice what comes to you and write it down
5.  Ask, "What would I love to create to feel this even more?"
6.  Notice what comes to you and write it down
7.  Repeat this process with the other three cores choices (choosing to be the predominant creative force, having health and vitality, and living your true nature and purpose).

This should take about three minutes per choice. This allows you to receive all the possibilities of how you already have the choice and how you can expand upon it.

From the lists you create, I want you just to notice what is really true for you. What makes you feel really great when you read it? Don't judge it. Just notice it, and put a circle around it.

I want you to find five to eight amazing end results you would love to create from what you have written. Here are some examples of end results that our workshop attendees have written down:

- I choose the end result of total financial abundance.
- I choose the end result of a happy and connected family.
- I choose the end result of becoming a therapist.
- I choose the end result of public speaking to large audiences.
- I choose the end result of building homes in South America.
- I choose the end result of an amazing, connected, and loving relationship with the man/woman of my dreams.
- I choose the end result of becoming an author.
- I choose the end result of owning my dream home.
- I choose the end result of healing animals with massage.
- I choose the end result of backpacking around the world.
- I choose the end result of writing children's books.
- I choose the end result of sprinting one hundred meters in under twelve seconds.
- I choose the end result of creating beautiful art.
- I choose the end result of starting a business.
- I choose the end result of a divine connection.

When you write down your end results, use the words, "I choose the end result." This is a powerful way to orientate to creative choice. In our workshops, we do a thirty-minute guided meditation on this process that really allows people to get out of their own way and receive what is true.

Here is a place to write down all your choices. Start with the first four core choices.

1. I choose to be the predominant creative force in my life.
2. I choose to love my life.
3. I choose health and vitality.
4. I choose to live my true nature and purpose.

Then, break it down into your more focused choices:

1. I choose the end result of _____.
2. I choose the end result of _____.
3. I choose the end result of _____.
4. I choose the end result of _____.
5. I choose the end result of _____.
6. I choose the end result of _____.
7. I choose the end result of _____.
8. I choose the end result of _____.

Don't focus on more than twelve at once. More can be too much.

After creating each choice, you can take each end result and define what the path ahead is. I like to focus on what could be done in the next ninety days to move towards this end result.

I like ninety days because it is a season, and there is a lot you can create in a season. Once you have the ninety-day outcomes, you can then decide what is needed to move forward on a monthly and weekly basis. I have found some people prefer to go from ninety days to thirty, and others like to go straight down to a week.

For some of your choices, there will be nothing you need to do in the next ninety days. If you get "there is nothing to do," let that be true. You don't always have to "do" something on every choice. Sometimes everything is in place, and you can just let that choice manifest perfectly. Many times in your relationship choice, it's as simple as one word like "time" or "love," and sometimes there is real work to be done to move that relationship towards what you desire.

Through using the Superconscious to decipher what you love, you are much more effective at creating because you are no longer creating two waves of information in the field. You have all your focus on just the one thing you desire to create, instead of half your focus on what you want and half your focus somewhere else.

In the past, you had "negative visions" disguised as goals. You were creating competing structures that interfered with each other. It's like throwing two stones into a pond—the ripples of each stone will interfere with the other and cause uneven waves. When you have a true end result, you put all your energy into one outcome, which creates just one strong wave of information or frequency.

By connecting to your Superconscious and deciphering what you would really love, you get outside of your current reality/understanding and enter a new place where you gain much more information. From here, you are able to formulate an action plan, using both your logical, grounded thinking and your emotional, creative genius to create amazing end results.

In the next chapter, we will talk about how to take these end results and bring them into reality. This is what we call the five steps of Superconscious Creation. It's time to learn the code and get the exact weekly and daily plan to bring all our end results into reality.

## CHAPTER 7 REVIEW

Most people don't go for what they love. Most people's goals are really negative visions and aren't true end results that they'd love.

A true end result is something you desire to create for no reason other than you would love to see it created. Being a Superconscious creator is about creating what you love!

Breaking your big vision down through lenses allows the structure to flow. If you just complete your day, it bundles into your week and your month, and then eventually, the end result is manifested. This is Superconscious creating.

The creation starts off by claiming the biggest end results you have and then letting the Superconscious guide you to what is there. When you learn to get information from the field, life will never be the same again.

# CHAPTER 8

# THE FIVE-STEP SUPERCONSCIOUS CREATOR CODE

Now it's time to bring it all together through one succinct process that takes fifteen minutes a day. You will be able to predictably create the reality you desire.

To be a creator is to understand the creation process. In nature, we observe that there are three major stages in the creation process: Germination, Assimilation, and Completion.

Every complete creative process moves through this cycle and always in the same sequence. The cycles are as natural and organic as the human birth cycle and have the same stages.

Germination occurs at conception. This is the prime initiating act that starts the entire process. Germination begins with excitement and newness. Think about a new relationship or a new idea. They're always exciting at the beginning.

Assimilation is often the least obvious phase of the process. In this phase, the initial thrill is gone. This phase moves from a focus on internal action to external action.

In this phase, you begin to have insights, ideas, connections, and added momentum. Your creation begins to take shape. It becomes more and more tangible. In this phase, you are always met with dissatisfaction and "failure," but with each action, you learn and gain specific skills.

Completion is the final stage when the creation comes to maturity. Few people have mastered this stage. Most tend to keep moving the goalpost farther and farther away. The initial goal has been doubled or quadrupled.

To create, you must be able to receive the full fruits of your labor. When you are creating, you are the only one who is able to declare a result as complete. You alone can determine when reality satisfies your vision.

Many people love the germination or idea phase. It is new, fun, and exciting. However, there is no risk at this stage. You haven't had to follow through with assimilation and bring the idea of a new relationship, healthy body, or business to completion.

Remember, completion often means a previous identity needs to die.

As your end result becomes more sold in reality, your self-sabotaging identity becomes more protective.

So, the germination stage often moves along nicely until we reach the assimilation phase, where we face resistance. We need to make sure the psychological tension created by the identity does not outdo and distract the process.

The " not a good enough" person starts focusing on how they need to be better. The perfectionist tries to avoid any "failure." The "not capable" person enrolls in a new course, and the victim blames others.

No matter what distraction you face, you need to follow-through! You must master your own creative process and stay in the end result.

Follow-through is not sexy. It's easier to allow your feelings to get the better of you and buckle at psychological tension.

If you do this, you will oscillate. When I hear people justify why they are not following through, they say:

"I knew it wasn't the right idea."

"It's just not the right time."

"I need to learn more."

"They weren't right for me."

"I just can't _____."

If you want to be a creator, you must follow through.

Even in the face of a current reality that doesn't look anything like what you desire, you must follow through.

If it was meant to be, it was because you created it. You, as the creator, made it happen.

If you want to have a successful business, you must keep going after a setback.

If you want a successful relationship, you have to get out and meet people.

If you want a best-selling book, you must write (and

continue to write even when your editor gives you disappointing feedback).

If you want to make sales, you must call people.

Thirteen years ago, I learned a lesson about follow through when I tried to establish a Mexican restaurant. I found a location and had a bank loan approved. At the last minute, the real estate agent called to say they had given the location to someone else.

I was devastated. I thought it was everything. It was perfect.

I told Deas I was giving up. It obviously was not meant to be after six months of organizing, planning, hiring the right chef, obtaining bank loans, business partners, and more. It was just too much.

He looked at me and said, "If that's all it took for you to give up, you really didn't want it, did you?"

He was right.

Laughing at me, he told me this setback was "nothing compared to what I will face in the future."

I never forgot Deas' words: "If this was all it took for you to give up, did you really want it?"

The answer was no.

His words changed my life, and I hope they change yours, too.

If you really want it, you will follow through.

But remember, you must follow through on the right end results!

I never started the restaurant because it wasn't what I truly desired. I needed to find my true end results.

You need to find them, as well. Dreams deserve to be experienced in this reality.

Deas died when a truck swerved across the center line and took him out on his motorbike. You never know if today will be your last. So, focus on what you decide to create and follow through.

Half a decade later, Deas' death became a catalyst for me to commit to creating a life I love. To choose to have it now and create what I love. I choose to focus on the end result and love the journey. I choose to be a heart-centered maniac on a mission and in love with life, creating amazing outcomes. I just decided, and I followed through.

Now it's your time to make a decision—to become a powerful Superconscious creator.

Welcome to a new reality.

## THE SUPERCONSCIOUS-CREATOR CODE

The five-step creation process should be done as a daily practice. It allows you to follow the wisdom process and get instructions for each of your choices in ten to fifteen minutes each day. This is so that all of your true choices are flowing.

If you have ten true choices, then you can do two per day to ensure you do the process for each choice at least once a week.

The five steps are:

1. Choose an end result you would love to create.
2. Create a structural tension with the current reality.
3. Step into the feeling of having it.
4. Recode resistance.
5. Take aligned action and follow through.

# —THE—
# 5 STEPS
## TO CONSCIOUSLY CREATE YOUR DESIRE

### 1. CHOOSE A TRUE GOAL
Align your target with your end result and move forward with complete clarity.

### 2. CREATE STRUCTURAL TENSION
Pull yourself toward what you desire without internal struggle and with minimal effort.

### 3. EMOTION OF END RESULT
Create NEW emotional set points based on the person you want to be rather than the person you need to fix.

### 4. UNPLUG AND RECODE
Replace old habits, beliefs, and feelings with new ones and step into your new reality with a deep understanding of your limits.

### 5. TAKE ALIGNED ACTION
Align your actions with your True Goal to create unparalleled momentum and remove the fear of "getting it wrong."

These are the five steps to create anything you desire, from health to relationships, wealth, and everything else.

By using this system, you truly can have it all. It will only take fifteen minutes a day, and it will allow you to create without the struggle.

By following these five steps, you will ensure you are in a creative structure, creating what you love and using your Superconscious to its full capacity to gain insight and Recode instructions.

These five steps allow you to create a focused vessel for your Superconscious to work in and then allow you to take the perfect action to manifest with ease. Let's get into it.

In the previous chapter, we got clear on true end results that you would love to create. This may have seemed like a giant step, and it definitely was; however, knowing your true end results is very important. But this isn't the hard part. The hard part is following through on what you get.

As you follow the Superconscious creation code, you give your thoughts and feelings less power and follow through on the information you get from the field. It becomes easier the more you do it because your resistance to following your intuition melts away more and more each time you do it.

Trust me; if you follow through on this process, you will witness miraculous results.

You will teach your Self-Conscious and Unconscious that listening to the Superconscious is a good thing and will turn down the extent of resistance. Over time, you will not need to Recode very often because all aspects of you will be happy to listen to the Superconscious and take action no matter what.

In this process, you get to be a creator. You get to have it all and be in love with creating more things you love. This is the reason why we are on this planet—to experience our creative energy and witness ourselves creating! You are always creating and always have been. Now you are deciding how and what to create.

It seems simple, but you may run into many problems at each step. Let's review how to be successful with each step. The following brings together everything discussed in previous chapters.

### I. CHOOSE AN END RESULT YOU LOVE AND GET THE NEXT ACTION

**The first step is to choose an end result you would love to create (like one of the core four). This ensures you are in creative focus.**

**You should have your true choices written down. Review them every ninety days, and focus on two choices a day.**

Many people go for true end results, but very few see them manifest predictably every time. The first mistake is not committing to a true end result. You must decide on the end result you would love to create. If you never make the decision, you can never have it.

The second mistake is trying to solve a problem by creating the end result. This always results in failure because as soon as you solve the problem, you have no need for the creation and, therefore, sabotage it.

The third mistake is making the creation too big or too small. If it's too big, you will feel overwhelmed at the size. If it's too small, it won't pull you through the tough challenges.

This is what lenses are for; start big, then break it down.

The fourth mistake is trying to control how it will show up. If you want financial abundance, let it show up in a gift, a business, or a suitcase lying on the street!

The fifth mistake is thinking you don't know what action to take or that you don't need to take *any* action. There is always an action to take. Sitting back and waiting for something to show up is still an action. However, most of the time, it's not an obvious action that will lead to the result you desire.

To review, this first step is all about tuning in to the end result you desire and deciphering the next action to take. At this point, you must already be living the core four orientation choices. If you are not, work on those first.

Remember, you can have anything you desire. It's just a choice, but you must move towards it. You must take action.

**Instruction for step one:** Decide on an end result you would love to create and write it down.

## 2. CREATE STRUCTURAL TENSION

**The second step is to create a measurement or structural tension with the current reality. We do this by asking, "Compared to that, where am I now?"**

Tension is what pulls everything together in this universe. When you learn to use creative tension, you will learn to harness a magical force to pull what you desire towards you—and to pull yourself to it.

The only way to create tension is to have two or more points that are in connection. We need two points because this creates a clear path for the tension to resolve itself.

*Remember, tension seeks resolution along the path of least resistance.*

When you create a measure of where your creation is now compared to where you would like it to be, you invoke the magnetic force called tension. By creating a disequilibrium, the structural tension wants to flow towards your end result.

You are not creating a competing wave; you are just completing a structure. The current reality and desired reality are not separate but joined by tension. Think of it as water at the top, middle, and end of a river. Even though they are in separate places, you wouldn't say they are disconnected, would you?

In the same way, your current reality is not separate from your desired reality. Each current reality is just a previous version of the desired end result, just like each point in the river is at a different point of getting to the sea.

It doesn't help to be negative about your current reality. Instead, observe where the creation is currently and think about it like you're painting a masterpiece. Maybe right now, it's a blank canvas, or maybe the canvas just got thrown out, and you're starting again. It doesn't matter—all current realities are in service of the end result you are creating. Simply observe the now and experience the natural tension, disequilibrium, or void between the now and the desire so you can experience momentum.

We must remember that we create it all. Sometimes, what looks like destruction is actually creating the space for what we really want to come through.

When working in this new structure, it's not uncommon for a person's reality to look like it is breaking down.

For example, someone might choose to have a loving relationship and step into the end result every day, filling themselves with love. Then all of a sudden, they find out their spouse has cheated. It looks like their life is falling apart, but is it?

What really happened?

When they shifted into a true end result of love and support, they no longer had the same need for old emotions like feelings of unworthiness, which they got from their current relationship. Because the partner was part of this structure, they were driven to find a way to make you feel unworthy again (because their Unconscious is trying to keep everything the same).

At this point, the person can choose to have the partner

align with a true choice of the loving relationship and do the work. Or, they can find a new partner who does align with the new version of themselves that feels love and fulfillment. The cheating partner was a needed step to create the true end result.

Again, the current reality sometimes has to break down for you to recreate a new future.

I once worked with a woman whose son was on drugs. She decided to raise happy and healthy children and stop reacting to his rebellion, but two weeks later, the son overdosed.

This actually ended up being the awakening the son needed. Because she didn't react to his rebellion, they could start over with a relationship built on creation instead of reaction.

These are very extreme examples, but they show the principle. It's not uncommon for someone to be creating financial abundance and lose their job. Someone creating health and vitality can be swiftly hit with symptoms of an underlying illness.

In these cases, the current reality becomes a seed of the future creation.

In review, to create the structural tension, we must observe what we have created now in relationship to what we desire.

We observe what is here and set up the disequilibrium of energy to resolve itself to complete what we desire.

**Instruction for step two:** Write down where you are now compared to the end result. What have you created compared to the end result?

### 3. STEP INTO THE EMOTION OF THE END RESULT

**The third step is to connect emotionally with your end result by stepping into the emotion of having it now.**

This way, you instruct the unified field of all possibilities where you desire to go and what you are choosing. It is as simple as stating, "I choose the end result of health and vitality," and then witnessing/visualizing with your eyes closed what it would be for that to be true.

To bring your end result to life, you need to gather the emotion of having it. By doing so, you teach your Unconscious what and how it must be now, so there is no resistance. Transformation and healing occur when you become it now.

Remember that everything is created twice. By stepping into your end result and feeling the emotion of it completed, you are creating a second feeling to the same end result.

Using this simple principle, you can create huge internal transformations and become the end result before it is made manifest. You can literally transform your body and identity by creating a different internal environment.

The only way to be in emotional alignment and to have no identity resistance is in the now. How you feel now = how you feel in the future.

So, how would you actually feel if you had the new car?

Or a new house?

Or if you were completing a huge goal?

You would feel exactly as you did the last time you created something. You wouldn't feel any different than yourself. Maybe, for a moment, you will feel something else, but overall, you will be the same. When you really get into the emotion of the end result, you can feel it, and you won't necessarily have a crazy super high feeling. You will simply feel the feeling of having it.

In review, if something is coded up in your reality to give you a feeling that you are not living or not allowed, you will not have it. If you have not "practiced having it," you will unconsciously avoid it or sabotage it. This is why I recommend using the emotion of the end result daily for every one of your choices. By going into the emotion of the end result, you instruct your body to know what you desire and to know it's safe to feel that way.

**Instruction for step three:** Close your eyes and witness yourself having the end result now. Allow it to be real. Then visualize yourself doing and completing the next action and feeling good about it (this should take no longer than a minute, but usually thirty seconds).

## 4. RECODE RESISTANCE

**The fourth step is to remove any resistance in the way.**

First, you ask, "What is in the way?" When you do that, resistance is pushed into the active experience, ready for you to Recode it.

Once you have allowed the resistance to pop into the active experience, you can connect to the Superconscious and Recode the instructions it gives.

In a perfect world, you would have a goal and then be able to go for it. You will get there. For most of us, we have an identity with certain unwanted beliefs, which produces resistance to taking the necessary action.

As you know, resistance is the opposing force to releasing the tension. For many people, fear of their unwanted beliefs coming true stops all movement.

Instead of going for what we want, we find ourselves pulled by the psychological tension and move in a different direction.

When you have true end results that you'd really love to create and you have stepped into the creative structure, your identity predictably resists. It doesn't want to change. So, in entering a new structure, you "pop" resistance into your active experience and uncover it.

Once you discover what is in the way, you then get to step into the Superconscious field and CHANGE the instructions. Remember, all resistance is just information that was useful in the past. Once all the resistance is neutralized, you get to INSTALL the end result emotions again.

You let go of what you don't want, giving the Unconscious new orientation instructions.

The three simple steps to removing all limitations are: 1—Uncover, 2—Change, 3—Install.

You don't want to just sit and ask, "What do I need to change?" or "What is wrong with me?" We cannot change what happened, and we do not need the things that happened to poison our future, so we want to let them go.

What you desire is at the end of the river, and your Unconscious has created blocks to stop the flow. When we get into the creative structure, we're 100 percent happy in the now and know what we desire to create; we can change the instructions and treat all the blocks by connecting to the Superconscious by simply asking. When we do this, we separate the information and emotion that caused the blocks.

When we do the Recode, many people get physical sensations and experience profound shifts, while others feel nothing. However, everyone notices that, for some strange reason, behaviors that used to be difficult are now easy. Everyone reports they can easily flow towards what they really desire.

Neuroscience has proven to us that our brain is "plastic" and can change its structure. In fact, this is how learning takes place. New connections can be made, and old ones can be reconsolidated or reorganized. If you would like more information on neuroplasticity, read Norman E. Doidge's books, *How the Brain Heals* and *The Brain That Changes Itself.*

Remember, as you go for what you want, you will come up against your own resistance. Once it is uncovered, use the Superconscious Recode process to release all the old patterns so action can occur.

Remember, you are a creative energy, and you created it all. Own the resistance, which was useful at one time, and Recode it.

Here are some open-ended questions you can use to uncover your resistance:

- What do I believe I have to be, do, or have in order to create the end result or take the best action?
- What do I believe about myself in relation to creating this end result?
- What do I believe about the end result?
- What emotions stop me?
- How am I defining myself in relation to the end result?
- What am I assuming?
- Where am I giving the power?
- What would I have to risk being true if I went for the end result?
- What internal conflicts do I have about the end result or the action?

These questions trigger the Unconscious into sharing its coding. It's like seeing all the rocks in the way of the flowing stream. Once you can see them, you can move them. Now the Superconscious needs to do the next step, which is to change the instructions.

I like to create a measurement of how much resistance there is. This allows you to remember where you were before you started so you can see the change at the end.

So, if 10/10 resistance is like swimming upstream, and 0/10 is an easy float downstream to your end results, how would you rate the level of resistance? Write that down.

To change the instructions, you simply connect to your Superconscious by dropping into your heart or stepping into innocence and asking for the treatment. Once you have asked for the change, simply get out of the way and notice what is different.

I usually say something like, "Superconscious, do you see this resistance to the end result? Can you please treat it perfectly?"

Once I ask for the change, I let go, surrender, and ask myself, "What is different?"

I love to witness the difference and experience the change. After a few minutes, I may ask for more change, or I may simply move on to the last part, which is to install the new emotion or way. I desire my Unconscious to orient, so there is no resistance to what I am creating.

Through installing, you will have no problem experiencing the end result to be true. So, close your eyes, step into the end result, and feel it.

When I do Superconscious Recode sessions, I sometimes have up to 1,000 people on a live call. Many are doing this for the first time, and I am constantly swept away by their responses. Many people feel huge shifts, energy flowing in and around their bodies, and some also fall asleep (only to wake up minutes later). Others feel nothing, are unsure of the change, and feel like they "missed out." Whatever is true for you is just perfect.

The only thing that matters is whether or not the resistance to your end result has shifted. If you are able to take an action or think about a situation and not feel old limiting feelings or thoughts, then that is perfect.

You know a Recode has worked when whatever was stopping you from moving towards your end result is no longer a problem. You are not sitting still, asking what is wrong with you, and trying to fix that. Instead, you are in momentum, moving towards a result that you would love, and you are aligning with that.

**Instruction for step four:**

1. Uncover resistance using questions.
2. Own the fact that you are Superconscious and created this resistance.
3. Go into your heart/innocence.
4. Connect to the Superconscious.
5. Command to treat the current coding.
6. Visualize and experience the end result as if it's happening now to install the emotion of it.


## 5. TAKE ALIGNED ACTION

**The fifth step is to take action towards your new manifestation.**

Without any resistance, you are able to take the required action and turn your thoughts into reality!

You are always in action, and in order to create, you must follow through on all instructions from the Superconscious.

If you don't follow through, you are giving an invisible command to all aspects of your Superconscious that you really don't want the end result, and you do not value the connection to the Superconscious. If you do not follow through, you will end up creating chaos.

The obvious action is the easiest and most natural way for the manifestation to occur. When you commit to an end result and engage your Superconscious, it is a very powerful structure.

I have learned from experience to trust the obvious action and follow through (no matter how much my Self-Conscious doubts it).

If there is no resistance, then the obvious action can be taken. If you want something, go for it.

It's that simple.

Action is the highest form of communication, and once you have Recoded all your resistance, you are free to move towards what you desire. And because you are in the right structure, you will turn your current reality into your desired one.

Unfortunately, many have told you the Law of Attraction works by you sitting back, doing nothing, and just receiving, and then everything turns up for you.

Just having a seed doesn't guarantee a forest. You must plant the seed, nurture it, and face setbacks. If there is a natural disaster, you will need to replant it. You will need to keep taking the correct action until you have what you set out to create. You must follow through to completion.

You cannot build your life on the premise that if you just think about what you desire and feel it, it will somehow show up.

There is always an action to take, and you only have two options when it comes to deciding the next action. You either know what to do and do it, or you do not know and must find out what you should do next. In either case, there is action to take.

It's also helpful to keep in mind that there are two types of action: masculine and feminine. In society, we generally think of masculine action as "action" and feminine action as "inaction." This is not true; they are simply different forms of action.

Masculine action is hunting, planting seeds, and going after what you want.

Feminine action is nurturing the seeds, harvesting, and receiving what comes back.

Both are needed!

Many people (like myself) get stuck in one of the two poles

of action. If you stay in the masculine and go after things all day without nurturing or receiving, you will end up exhausted.

If you try to stay with the feminine action of self-care, surrender, and receiving all day without the masculine, you will not create anything. You'll need someone else to do the creation/decision-making for you.

You need both!

All great things have small beginnings. Every masterpiece has its first brushstroke. Every building has its first brick, and every life its first breath. The same rule is true for nearly every aspect of our world, and our personal success is no exception.

Small actions compound to create huge results. This is the power of compounding.

Consider "the domino effect." On its own, a domino isn't much. It's about two inches tall and weighs about as much as a small box of matches. But with the domino comes a force.

In fact, one domino has the capacity to knock down another piece that is 1.5x larger. This seemingly infinitesimal ability compounds to produce incredible outcomes.

Imagine a long string of dominos lined up one after the other, each one progressively 1.5x larger than the last. If you were to knock down the first two-inch domino, you would set off a chain reaction that, by the fifty-seventh iteration, would produce enough force to knock over a domino stretching the distance between the earth and the moon.

**Instruction for step five:** Ask your Superconscious to give you instructions. Ask, "What are all the possible actions I could take to turn this end result into reality?" Write them down and follow through on one of them.

That's it! Use the Five-Step Process outlined in this chapter every day.

Remember to start with the core four choices and then have other choices (up to twelve). I have a business choice, a family choice, a relationship choice, a fun choice, a financial choice, and an impact choice (along with a couple of others).

Choose one or two to focus on every day. Step into the end result every day. Recode any resistance every day. And take the obvious action every day. If you do this every day, you will create amazing results in your life.

## CHAPTER 8 REVIEW

You must learn to become Superconscious, even when it is hard to follow through!

As you decide to follow through on the things that really matter to you, old patterns of information and decisions will pop into your active experience, causing resistance. You must learn to stay focused on the end results and "leave the baby crying."

The five steps to the Recode process are:

1. Choose an end result you would love to create.
2. Create a structural tension by noticing the current reality.
3. Step into the feeling of having it.
4. Recode resistance.
5. Take aligned action and follow through.

When choosing the correct action, what is most important is just to choose one and start. We very rarely get the action right the first time, so take your best guess and follow through. You will quickly learn whether or not it's taking you to where you desire.

The only way to be in emotional alignment and have no identity resistance is in the now.

How you feel now = How you feel in the future. We use the emotion of the end result to understand what we must align with now.

Sometimes the current reality has to break down for you to recreate a new future.

You must stay focused on your end result, notice the current reality, and accept that this was your creation. It's a seed of the future creation, and it is perfect. Love the now. It's just a step in this journey called life, and every moment is precious.

You have the ability to let go of and reconstruct all aspects of your neurobiology. You just need a way to connect to the part of you that's doing the creating and create new instructions.

To create, you must follow through on all instructions from the Superconscious. If you don't follow through, you are giving an invisible command to all aspects of your Super-conscious that you don't really want the end result.

There are three major stages in the creation process: Germination, Assimilation, and Completion.

Every complete creative process moves through this cycle and always in the same sequence. The cycles are as natural and organic as the human birth cycle and have the same stages.

# GAME TIME

Now that you have come to the end of this book, it's time for you to get out there and turn your biggest loves into reality, to have it all, and to create more of what you love. What a life!

You have the key to unlock your Magnetic Mind and become the powerful, creative force that you are. You are Superconscious. You are the creative energy that collapses all potentials and possibilities into a human form.

You went through individuation and created an Unconscious orientation to a problem you thought you needed to overcome. Through this process, you forgot you have unlimited possibilities and only saw limitations.

You forgot you were the powerful creator, and you orientated to the world as a powerless victim. Now it's time to stop, to realize you can have it all now, reconnect to your Superconscious, and change all the instructions using the five steps of the Recode.

You're tuned in to big end results that you love.

You've stepped into them and felt them.

You've created structural tension.

You've uncovered and Recoded all resistance and know how to take aligned action.

In short, you've learned to regain your power and create a life you love!

Please commit to doing the Superconscious Creator Code every day.

Start by having the true end results that you choose written out.

"I choose the end result of _____."

Then each day, go through the five steps to clear resistance and receive wisdom on exactly how to turn each choice into reality.

If you do two to three choices a day, you will get through each choice at least once a week. That's all it takes to get into the right structure and create from your Superconscious.

I am so honored to share this information with you. Everything I have shared has changed my life profoundly, and I choose the same transformation for you.

We have many workshops and trainings happening all around the world and online. Please check out our website www.yourenotbroken.com for up-to-date times and locations. I hope to see you at one soon.

I'd also love to hear from you, so feel free to email me at hello@yourenotbroken.com. I endeavor to reply personally to every email, so please write me.

Remember, you are not broken. You are a powerful, Superconscious creator.

You create your reality.

Stay focused, stay magnetic, and do what matters most.

Love your friend,
Christopher M Duncan

P.S. The best way to change the world is to get this book

into as many hands as possible. What a great creation for upcoming birthdays, Christmas/other celebrations, or as a random gift. Thank you in advance for sharing this work with the people you love.

# ABOUT THE AUTHOR

**CHRISTOPHER MICHAEL DUNCAN** is a New Zealander who lives in the Gold Coast, Australia, with his wife, Harriet. After a near-death experience in 2009, he dedicated his life to understanding how to create success and find meaning in the laws of the universe.

What he discovered was that most people have been misled about the fundamental ways in which manifestation really works. After studying one-on-one with some of the most transformational minds in the world, Christopher created the magnetic mind method, teaching others how to become Superconscious and create anything they desire.

CPSIA information can be obtained
at www.ICGtesting.com
Printed in the USA
LVHW040353311022
731958LV00001B/123

9 781544 519432